"After a lifetime of studying optometry, I believe the idea here by Al are the critical business tools that every practitioner needs. If asked to recommend a book for practicing ODs and students, I would say, 'there are many excellent books but start with this one!'"

David Cockrell, OD
Past President,
American Optometric Association

"A must read for those who want to be successful in business and life. And for those who have achieved success, you will quickly identify with why you succeeded! I only wish it would have been available to me when I graduated from optometry school."

Ron Blum, OD
Inventor, Entrepreneur,
and Cleinman Performance Partners' First Client

"With this book, Cleinman brings together not just a large collection of eminently sensible suggestions and nuggets of advice to independent optometrists. With his insights, he also helps elevate practices that embrace these skills to a higher level of professionalism and toward the achievement of exceptional customer experiences. People skills, running the business by the numbers (my personal favorite), creating a culture of trust and respect within the practice; it is all there. In my opinion, the book fills a huge void in the business education of independent optometry."

Tom Schinkel
International Business Consultant

"I challenge any OD who's looking to better their practice to get a copy of Mr. Cleinman's book, read it, and then launch some of the management pearls that are contained in it so that you can prosper and balance your practice and your life."

P. Herreras

"I'm not an optometrist, the targeted audience of the book, but as an owner of a small business, it was easy to be hooked into reading just one more chapter and then another as the message resonated and inspired. Many will read this book, all will learn from it, but the smart ones will act on the wisdom being shared and gain critical insight into how others in their field of endeavor make it look so easy!"

J.M.Y.

Just finished reading your book, [and] it made me realize what a great influence you have been on my career. I learned so much through the years from you, and I would not be where I am today without the help from you and your team. I am not sure you realize what an impact that you have had on our industry and on so many of us out in the trenches fighting the battle every day.

Richard Krzyzak, OD

Printed in the United States of America
Second Printing, 2017

ISBN Number 978-1-4951-6873-4

Cleinman Performance Partners, Inc.
343 Main Street
Oneonta, NY 13820
607.431.1001
www.cleinman.com

To my children — Gabe, Ashley, and Joe — who have always helped me to better understand perspective.

Table of Contents

PREFACE

I am a student of life. As long as I can remember, I have addressed each day and all that I observe with the eyes and curiosity of a youngster. I'm fascinated by experience and experiences; I collect experiences like some people collect coins. I love discussion and contrarian thinking. It is my belief that, through others' passionate perspectives, we can often see our own world with better clarity.

The great speaker Zig Ziglar once said, "Your attitude not your aptitude will determine your altitude."[1] I choose my attitude and I choose to be the luckiest man alive. Through my conscious daily choices, I uncover countless opportunities. I have always believed that "life is a banquet of possibilities" and it is up to me to discover and feast upon them. Unfortunately, I have also observed that the jaundice of years turns many into closed-minded "negaholics" afraid to open their eyes and minds to the opportunities that stare them squarely in the face. Success is largely about luck (and hard work), but it's not the result of being lucky. No, success is the result of choosing to be lucky; there's a big difference.

1 Zig Ziglar, "Your Attitude Not Your Aptitude," *Ziglar,* http://www.ziglar.com/quotes/your-attitude-not-your-aptitude.

It is from this perspective that I lay down the observations, ideas, and principles that follow. Having invested over 40 years in the eye care industry as an employee, entrepreneur, consultant, writer, and speaker, I believe that our industry is full of unprecedented opportunity. It is up to each of us to take advantage of all the amazing possibilities before us. In spite of the parasite called managed care, the headaches of being an employer, the challenges of the health care system, the impact of the Internet and disruptive technologies, the uncertainty of our economic times, and the stress of work/life balance — in spite of all the obstacles that are before us — optometry is an amazing profession. For many, it's a calling. In my opinion, becoming a private-practice optometrist represents the catbird seat to many riches.

But success doesn't come automatically with your diploma or by hanging out your shingle. Regardless of the school from which you graduated, odds are pretty good that you left your academic world suffering from a serious bout of "clue deficiency syndrome" (CDS) when it comes to business and leadership. I mean this with love in my heart, and I certainly don't imply any disrespect for your eight years of hard work or the many wonderful schools of optometry that produce professionals of the highest caliber. Optometrists are very well educated in the science of optometry. But what is also clear from my seat is that the vast majority of optometrists have little understanding of what it means to be *in the business of optometry*. That education comes only with time, experience, perspective, and an open mind. There are a few shortcuts, however, and, hopefully, this book will be considered one of them.

This is not your typical practice management tome. In the chapters ahead, you'll find ideas, observations, and insight taken from a lifetime focused on the business side of optometry — and from a life lived fully. Having personally worked with hundreds of very successful — and sometimes very troubled — optometrists, I believe there's little I haven't experienced as it relates to the business of optometry.

Yours is a complex profession for which I have infinite respect. I have not attempted to cover every management issue with this work, but I believe that I've touched on many critical aspects of what it takes for success both inside and outside the industry.

Throughout this book, I've taken real-world experiences and used them to drive specific points. I've changed names and some details for obvious reasons. With your open mind, I'm confident you'll uncover some lessons that will help you see your world with better clarity and realize all that you deserve from your chosen profession. Enjoy!

CHAPTER 1

It Starts with Values

Dr. Frank is 62. He owns a practice with revenue in the millions. He's made investments in real estate and other businesses, many of which have gone bust. He owns two homes. He's always had nice cars (usually leased). Everyone knows Frank; he belongs to two country clubs and eats out often. He maintains a high profile, moneyed persona. He's made millions — and spent every dime and then some. He's chased get-rich-quick schemes. He's been a philanderer. He's always looking to save money, whether through hard negotiations or outright arrogance. His employees have long ago lost respect for him. His family is in shambles. Vendors avoid his calls. When push comes to shove, Frank will throw anyone under the bus to protect his assets and his lifestyle. Now, on the cusp of retirement, Frank is about to go bankrupt.

Dr. Sam is 52. He owns a very successful practice that generates over $400,000 per year in earnings. He sees patients three days a week. He plays golf as often as he wants and travels several weeks each year on vacations with his wife. He owns his own building. He's a leader in his community and is sought for his wisdom. He hires the very best people, pays them well, and acknowledges their worth. Always searching for and sharing new ideas, Sam has forged relationships far and wide. He considers his vendors as partners and sits on the board of one of his suppliers. He's a successful stock trader and works at his hobby daily. Sam loans money to those in need and donates to area causes anonymously. Sam has a substantial nest egg and is debt free.

What's the difference between Frank and Sam? They're both ODs operating in similar communities, and they're even graduates of the same school. But, like the kid in the proverbial candy store, Frank is all about what's in front of him. Frank has an insatiable appetite for more. Frank is about stuff. His value system is determined by the Joneses — as in keeping up with. If you're between Frank and a goal, you're going to get stepped on. It's all about Frank. And after years of playing his game, the chickens are coming home to roost. Time's run out for Frank; he will likely retire a broke and broken man.

Sam, on the other hand, has always been concerned about others. Knowing that it's his staff that makes the difference, Sam has, for years, paid his team for 40 hours when they only work 38. He maintains health and retirement plans for his employees. They receive bonuses based on performance. Sam gives before receiving. He pays himself with what's left over from operating a successful business. He works hard and has fun. Sam will retire by age 60 (he could actually retire now) with all that he needs.

I've observed this same story on multiple occasions. The reason for Frank's challenges is pretty simple, in my opinion. You see, Frank doesn't know who he is. He has no value system. His got lost long ago in his quest for more. Sam, on the other hand, clearly knows who he is and what he values.

The long-term success of your practice will more largely depend on your value system than anything else. As the saying goes, "you can't fool mother nature." Before you even think about opening or acquiring your own practice, ask yourself some important questions: Who am I? What do I stand for? What do I want out of life? How will I define my success? What responsibilities do I have to others?

Why are you on this planet and who do you wish to be? It's not your business that's your primary concern, it's *you*. And without a clear destination in mind, without melding your personal values with your business interests, your business will not provide all that it could.

Your value system shouldn't be taken for granted. The exercise of clearly defining your values should be Job Number One, and it is likely long overdue. Some 30 years ago, I solicited the assistance of a friend to help me to clarify my values. We spoke at length about my views on trust, social responsibility, teamwork, ideas, etc. The result was a series of short statements that summarize what I believe. For example:

- Life is a banquet of possibilities. Seek and discover them. Feast upon them.

- We are all members of the same team — within our family, our community, our society, and within humanity. We will succeed only as the team succeeds. It's a big responsibility.

- People deserve our trust. What we sow, we reap tenfold.

My maxims have guided my personal and business dealings for my entire entrepreneurial life. They are mine — not adopted from some book, but from an exploration of my beliefs at the ripe age of 27. They are the touchstone against which I measure every act and action. They now reside in both my conscience and subconscious mind. And in those times when I've gotten upside down and backwards, as we all do from time to time, it's evident that it was because I wandered from these core values.

We can't live a perfect life, nor should we try. Who's to say what perfect is? But I have observed that those who lead extraordinary lives — those who are fulfilled and for whom luck always seems to be on their side — those are people who clearly know who they are, what they stand for, and what they want out of life. They're open to the possibilities that arise because they clearly know which of those possibilities are aligned with their values. They make decisions with greater ease. They don't waste time.

Take the time now to define your values. It's a worthwhile exercise. Make your life your life; you can't buy it in a box and it's not returnable for credit. To be safe (no disrespect to those who believe otherwise), you've got one shot at it. Don't leave your value system up to chance.

CHAPTER 2

Learning is a Lifelong Endeavor

Show me a successful optometrist and I'll show you a professional student. Certainly, continuing medical education (CME) is a requirement of licensure. But ask yourself these important questions: If CME was not a requirement of licensure, would you still invest the time and money? And when you do attend, do you really pay attention, or are you just there to get your ticket punched? Your responses to these questions signal your attitude towards learning and are, I believe, a potential predictor of your life's accomplishments.

I am astounded at the number of professionals who have never attended a personal or business development program. This is especially disconcerting when one considers that the typical professional has almost no training in the business side of their profession. Education doesn't stop with your diploma. Indeed, in my opinion, receipt of a cap and gown should be in celebration of a single step in a lifelong endeavor. Investing in yourself through ongoing personal development will greatly impact your life's success as well as provide a return on investment like no other.

A Different Perspective

I don't mean to imply that being a scholar has any connection with being economically successful. Indeed, I believe that the opposite is likely true; that many very successful entrepreneurs were actually pretty mediocre students in terms of classic scoring methodologies (for a variety of reasons, most having nothing to do with intelligence). But being academically bored is not necessarily the inverse of being a lifelong learner. I, for one, was completely turned off by the book-learning process yet have always been intensely curious. I believe that it is my curiosity and my investment in lifelong personal development that has provided the success I've enjoyed.

Curiosity — together with a healthy, competitive attitude — is the blood that flows through the veins of most successful individuals. Indeed, teaching curiosity and healthy competition at the earliest ages is critical to the success of our society. Curiosity is the means by which we attain breakthroughs, while competitiveness (not necessarily with others) is the driving force behind the work required for success in any endeavor.

It's interesting to observe this concept at work, and my wisdom-sharing membership organization, Cleinman Performance Network, provides us with an amazing laboratory. Who are the most successful participants? They are those members who come back year in and year out and who are committed to the process of personal development. These individuals invest two weekends a year in taking an "outside in" view of their businesses and themselves. They take their weekends seriously, but not so seriously that they don't have

16

fun in the process. They always have a positive attitude and they seek one or two good ideas that will take them to the next level. They understand that these ideas won't just appear; they have to work to obtain them. They also understand that persistent implementation is key to their success. They don't take the attitude of "I tried it and it doesn't work." Their attitude is always "tell me how it worked for you."

Successful optometrists invest energy in understanding what works for others, why it works, and how they can adapt these ideas to their own situations. They're always on a quest for knowledge, and they always share their insights. They invest the time necessary in the learning process. They read industry journals as well as business magazines and books. They attend workshops and trade shows, both inside and outside of the industry. They retain consultants to tap into the knowledge base of experience. They are innately curious.

Learning is no longer something done before age 25 after which one applies their learning to the workplace. Learning is a lifelong endeavor involving both formal and informal development processes. However, learning shouldn't be perceived as a destination as in "I need to learn this or that." Successful individuals consciously understand that learning is a process that needs to be acculturated within themselves and their organizations. It's all part of your life's investment.

CHAPTER 3

Success is from 5 to 9, not 9 to 5

I grew up in a tiny village in Upstate New York. My parents were the grocers in town, and they generally worked seven days a week from 7:00 a.m. to 7:00 p.m. Their biggest income year would have placed their earnings at somewhere just north of $9 an hour in today's dollars. They toiled at their trade for over 30 years, with my mother carrying on after my father's passing.

I remember the phone ringing one evening near eleven o'clock. "Helen (my mother's name), I don't have milk for the kids for breakfast; would it be too much trouble for you to open the store?" I watched my mom get re-dressed and head off to open the store for a two-dollar sale on which she would have made less than twenty cents.

My parents' store was, at times, the town coffee shop, community center, telephone booth, and babysitting service. On the side, my mother also owned an antique business in partnership with her sister. It was run daily by my grandmother who continued to work every day until she was in her late 80s. My father was always selling something door to door, be it shoes, greeting cards, or candy. On several occasions, when times were really tough, my father would take a hated factory job to make ends meet. When Webster searched for an example of the word frugal, my parents and grandparents were on the short list.

Literally starting with the money in their pockets, my parents built a business that worked for them. They raised five productive kids, purchased and maintained a modest home, supported a community and, while never even being close to middle class economically, led a highly independent life. My mother ultimately sold her small store for enough to fund a reasonable retirement when combined with her Social Security income and penny-pinching persona.

From my parents and grandparents, I learned how to work. And I learned that it isn't what you do during business hours that makes the difference, but what you do when everyone else isn't and when others wouldn't.

I learned the concept of WOW service from my parents: work hard and smart. Success is from 5 to 9, not 9 to 5.

In his book *Outliers: The Story of Success,* author Malcolm Gladwell poses a provocative question: "Why do some people succeed, living remarkably productive and impactful lives, while so many more never reach their potential?" While his answers are many and very surprising, one of the most insightful was his conclusion that success simply takes practice, which Gladwell identifies as about 10,000 hours.[1] Whether it was the Beatles or Bill Gates or a child prodigy, the author's research clearly showed that these individuals simply practiced more than others. They honed their craft for the equivalent of years before they arrived.

My dear, late friend Al Gallodoro, whom the great band leader Jimmy Dorsey called "the greatest sax player who ever lived,"[2] was a professional musician for more than 80 years. He continued to perform up to 10 days prior to his passing at age 95 and, in spite of his experience and skill, continued to practice for hours and hours daily!

With so much empirical data and observation about what it takes to be successful in any endeavor, I find it fascinating that, by my calculations, the average optometrist invests only about four hours a week actually working *on* their business. The rest of the time, in the words of *E-Myth's* Michael Gerber, "they're working 'in' their business"[3] doing the day-to-day technical work of being an optometrist. That's all well and good, but is it then any wonder why the average optometrist owns a job, not a business? Why toil daily seeing patients or waiting for patients to come see you if you can earn more with less effort working for someone else? But, as my parents proved to me long ago, "It's not about the money — it's about your independence." What would

---

1 Malcolm Gladwell, *Outliers: The Story of Success* (New York: Little, Brown and Company, 2008).

2 Peter J. Levinson, *Tommy Dorsey: Livin' in a Great Big Way: A Biography* (Cambridge: Da Capo Press, 2005).

3 Michael E. Gerber, *The E-myth Physician: Why Most Medical Practices Don't Work and What to Do About It* (New York: HarperBusiness, 2003).

happen if you worked as hard on the business of optometry as you do on the profession?

What separates the high performers (which my firm defines as optometrists who generate over $750 per hour) from the average (about $250 per hour)? I can summarize it in a few words: these individuals understand who they are, they understand what they want, and they're willing to work to attain it. Nothing in life worth having comes easy. Your diploma is not a guarantee of success; it's a ticket to the game. What you're willing to do — what you're willing to sacrifice — will determine your ultimate outcome. Are you willing to see a patient on a Sunday evening? To work the Rotary breakfast at 6:00 a.m. on a Saturday? To toil late into the night writing out the agenda for next week's staff meeting? To cut the grass yourself to save $50 that would be better invested in a brochure for your practice? Are you willing to postpone the new car and the fancy home? Are you willing to make sacrifices to achieve your goals? Take a look at your credit card balances and you may find the answer.

Right about now, you may be saying to yourself that you're going to go about achieving success in a different way; you're going to work smarter, not harder. Well, there's certainly some logic in that. Yes, you should be reading others' success stories, interacting with successful peers and seeking, as we've discussed in a prior chapter, to borrow ideas wherever you can. Ideas and methodologies are readily transferred, but ideas and methodologies are a dime a dozen. Implementation is the key, and implementation requires hard work — lots of it. And the odds are pretty high that you have little experience at it relative to business.

Tiger Woods and Michael Jordan, both wildly successful athletes, didn't just jump unprepared into a game or match. They were known for shooting hoops into the wee hours or for driving ball after ball after ball at the practice range. They knew it takes practice to be a pro and that there were literally hundreds of other athletes waiting in line to knock them off their game. They worked smart, for sure. But their success lies in implementation, and implementation takes work.

Dr. Ron has a $500,000 practice that he opened cold 15 years prior. Each month, his staff diligently sends out recall notices to patients, informing them that it's time for their annual eye exam. Each month, Dr. Ron hopes that the phone will ring and that appointments will be booked. During the last recession, he saw a dramatic falling off of his appointment schedule, and even now he's experiencing a decline in revenue. Patients simply aren't calling.

Dr. John has a $1.2 million practice that he opened in a very similar community about 40 miles from that of Dr. Ron at just about the same time. With each appointment, Dr. John informs his patients of their need for an annual exam and his staff books pre-appointments with 90 percent of the patients that Dr. John sees. Each month, Dr. John knows with pretty solid certainty what he can expect in revenue based on his pre-appointment system. During the last recession, he actually experienced growth, as he has every year since he's been in practice.

At a recent gathering, I learned that Dr. Ron and Dr. John were introduced to the concept of annual pre-appointment at the same workshop some 10 years prior. When asked why he hadn't implemented the system, Dr. Ron responded, "We tried it and my staff didn't like it so it didn't work." Dr. John's retort was, "Yeah, we had the same result initially, and it took us a couple of years to work the bugs out."

This is an example of the power of persistence. I am not suggesting that success is about all work and no play. Nor am I suggesting that one can't be successful and live a balanced life. What I am saying is that being successful at anything isn't guaranteed and, more than ideas and education, success takes hard work and persistence. That's why it's so important to be passionate about your work. First, because you're going to be an optometrist for a long time. Second, because being a successful optometrist requires a lot of work, so you'd better find out what aspects of the profession you really enjoy and focus on those while delegating to others, as best you can, those aspects of the role that you don't enjoy. What specialties really get your blood flowing? What tasks do you abhor? Make a list. Explore. When you find your groove, you will not resent the hard work necessary for success. We can't always outsmart our competition, but we can outwork them.

CHAPTER 4

Surround Yourself with Smart People

Doctors provide solutions. They provide answers. But successful CEOs actually operate in the inverse. When you put on your CEO hat, your job is not to provide solutions but to ask questions and make decisions. In order to ask questions, you must have a team (both inside and out) that can provide you with recommendations. As a doctor, it is your job to know all that you can possibly know about your patient's needs. But as a CEO, your job is to know what questions to ask and to identify those individuals who can provide you with the answers you need to make a sound decision. Because the knowledge required to be successful in business is remarkably diverse and is increasing at almost warp speed. As business becomes more complicated, you must surround yourself with many resources. You simply can't go it alone.

The Universe of Knowledge

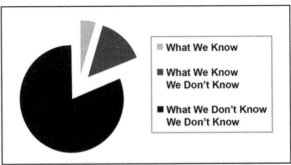

As the chart above indicates, what we actually know is a very small part of the universe of knowledge. While understanding what we know we don't know is a critical component of decision making, it's what we don't know we don't know that will always bite us. Successful individuals are quick to surround themselves with the resources necessary to cover the knowledge that they're missing. It's far more efficient and effective to develop these resources than to attempt to learn what you need to know yourself.

If they are to be successful, leaders need a well-trained, very smart group of people who can handle the projects and tasks that the leader can't or doesn't want to handle. Additionally, they need people with whom they can consult when making decisions, to whom they can turn for advice, and to whom they can delegate the decision making. These may include accountants, consultants, attorneys, counselors, politicians, and others.

A Different Perspective

John is a friend of mine — a very successful college professor and consultant. He often asks a thought-provoking question when he greets me (and, I assume, others): "Who have you met lately that's interesting?" It's a great conversation starter. But what John is also doing is collecting contacts. John's network of contacts is wide and deep, and when he needs information, he knows where to find it.

You are only as good as the people around you. Successful leaders know this. That's why they are collectors of individuals. Whether it's recruiting for employees or for a contact that may come in handy at a later date, these leaders exhibit an innate curiosity about others and are always collecting business cards from individuals with whom they come in contact. They preserve and nurture these contacts, recognizing that someday they may need those individuals.

The same applies to recruiting employees. We know that, no matter what we do, we will likely lose an employee or two this year. This will come as the result of many things outside of our control, such as parenthood, relocation of a spouse, etc. Successful leaders recognize this and are in a constant hunt for potential employees. Recruiting becomes second nature. Add to your arsenal a tool like the business card shown and you'll be amazed how many good people you'll identify and how many new patients you'll secure.

You've Impressed Me.
If you are ever seeking an employment opportunity,
please contact me directly about our current openings.
We'd love the opportunity to discuss our practice and
explore how we might work together.

John Smith, OD

John Smith, OD
Advanced Eyecare   222 Main Street

201-555-1212
Anytown, NY 12345

CHAPTER 5

You Are the Brand

It was a cold Chicago day about 25 years ago. I was attending a contact lens seminar. At the end of the program, during the question-and-answer session, a doctor stood up and loudly voiced in a frustrated tone to the speaker: "I'm sick and tired of it! How am I supposed to compete when the guy down the street is selling contacts for $39.95?"

The speaker attempted to allay this doctor's frustrations with some tactical suggestions. Being the quiet, reserved individual that I am, I felt compelled to add to the conversation.

"Doctors," I said, "Your challenge is not the guy down the street selling contacts for less than you can buy them. Your challenge is deciding what you sell. You don't sell contacts. You sell *you*. And I can't get *you* down the street."

My message about branding is quite simple. First, you must understand the meaning of brand and your role as a brand leader. I'm a firm believer that building and maintaining a brand is a key component in the success of any business whether it's an optometry practice, coffee shop, or manufacturer. I also believe that you, as the practice leader, are the "keeper of the brand."

But before you can understand your role as keeper of the brand, you must have a clear understanding of the definition of brand. Your practice's brand is defined by the total experience your patients have with your practice — from their first interaction (an advertisement, press release, or referral) to the end of the transaction (a thank you note, follow-up phone call, etc.). Your brand is defined by everything that the patient experiences. Everything. How you and your staff walk, talk, and present are significant elements of your brand. Your physical space impacts your brand. Your stained ceiling tiles and photocopied forms impact your brand. Everything!

> "A brand is the set of expectations, memories, stories, and relationships that, taken together, account for a consumer's decision to choose one product or service over another."[1]

Consider that your competition — whether a chain, fellow independent, vision plan, internet purveyor, or big-box retailer — largely sells the same stuff as you. Everyone has frames, lenses, and contacts, and the consumer has little understanding of the difference in products. Yes, you may package your product in a unique way or sell some product lines that others don't. You may even provide some specialized services like low vision, dry eye, or vision development. But those are only tools in the game

---

1 Seth Godin, "define: Brand," *Seth's Blog* (blog), December 13, 2009, http://sethgodin.typepad.com/seths_blog/2009/12/define-brand.html.

of competition and, unless you promote yourself in such a way that your desired consumer clearly understands the difference, you're thrown into the same pot as all other competitors. In reality, there is little that separates you from your competition unless you educate your consumer. But you do have secret brand weapons — tools that no one else has:

- You

- Your team

- Your physical environment

- Your patient experience

Most marketers, when asked to assist you with your practice, will focus on developing a physical image (such as a logo) or some cute and perceived memorable message ("Eye Care Because We Care"). This approach might have worked in the mass-media era when you could buy patients for a bit of advertising investment. But I think this kind of approach is largely a waste of energy in today's world unless you build your brand image first on the proper platform. In today's wired world where consumers communicate with thousands of other consumers directly through such social media platforms as Facebook and Yelp, a cute logo isn't going to cut it. Why? Because, in a word, such approaches are fake.

"People don't buy what you do, they buy why you do it."[2]

2 Simon Sinek, *Start with Why: How Great Leaders Inspire Everyone to Take Action* (New York: Portfolio, 2009).

You have a unique brand story that should be based upon why you became an optometrist to begin with. Now, while some readers will confess that they became an OD because they didn't want to go to school for eight more years to become an MD or because they didn't want to be on 24-hour call, the majority of you have a real and often heart-felt reason for joining the profession. Dig for it and share it. Work with a marketing professional to identify your unique story and communicate it. Develop your elevator speech so that you can impart your brand story in 30 seconds. Then eat, sleep, breathe, walk, and talk your brand.

> "If the consumer (whether it's a business, a buyer, a voter or a donor) doesn't pay a premium, make a selection, or spread the word, then no brand value exists for that consumer."[3]

Are you confident that patients will pay a premium for your services and make referrals to your practice? If not, perhaps you should take a hard look at what you're selling.

Here are some practical tests to help you assess your brand position. With this quick quiz, you will reveal opportunities to take action that will help insulate you from those who simply sell hard goods.

1. Can I consistently communicate my desired brand position in thirty seconds or less?

For example, your answer may be, "When I was just entering first grade, we discovered that I had a challenge reading. My

---

3 Godin, "define: Brand."

parents, who were both teachers and very education centric, were rightfully concerned. They took me to an optometrist who was very caring and who helped me with selecting the right eyewear and obtaining some specialized vision training to overcome my learning challenge. Over the course of a year, he and his staff worked closely with me and made a significant difference in my life. I was so impressed with his care and attitude towards my needs that I chose to follow in his footsteps. I love my profession because vision impacts virtually everything we do, and I deeply desire to help my patients get all that they can out of life. That's why our practice, in addition to providing general and medical optometry services, specializes in assisting with learning and development."

2. Do you hire staff members who support your desired brand?

As an example, it would make a great deal of brand-building sense if the hypothetical OD described above hired only staff members who were either former teachers or who have some form of vision need. Certainly, a caring personality profile would be mandatory. All too often, we see a disconnect between a client's desired brand and the staff they have hired to deliver their brand promise.

3. Is your visual identity up to date?

Every successful brand keeps its visual identity fresh — sometimes with changes that are so subtle they can hardly be noticed. Make sure that the visual identity of your brand looks current. Here are some simple rules of thumb:

- Keep your staff looking sharp by developing and executing a consistent look. How your staff dresses plays an important role in the development of your brand image. I am not a fan of classic scrubs, as they connote a negative experience (hospitals and the presence of bodily fluids). While I know many optometrists feel that scrubs present a medical image, I believe you can express that message in a much more positive way (for instance, with short white lab coats). Provide your team with an adequate clothing allowance that provides for new uniforms frequently (perhaps quarterly). Don't wait until clothes look worn or the colors are out of date.

- Redecorate your reception area and optical boutique approximately every three years. The changes don't have to be drastic, but replacing carpeting, seating or upholstery, and wall décor gives you an opportunity to use fashionable colors and make a fresh statement about the practice.

- Reconsider your logo and exterior signage. Most practices put up their signs and forget about them. If it's been longer than five years, they may be out of date. Your signage is an important element of delivering a first impression. Make sure it's a good one.

4.   Is your product keeping pace?

By product, I mean everything you do, including eye health and vision services as well as eyewear products — the whole shebang. Do you offer the latest technology and eye care services? Is your product line distinctive, and is it offered in the most patient-pleasing environment? Can your patients obtain what you sell on the Internet or down the street, leaving you vulnerable to price shopping? Are you utilizing the latest in technology, or is your instrumentation old and tired? Every time a patient visits your office, you should be able to demonstrate something new to them, be it a new product line or a new examination technology.

5.   Is your patient base aging?

Sometimes patients grow old with a brand (and an eye doctor). While it's great they stick with you, you must also continue to attract new customers/patients to your brand. What are you doing to attract and keep younger patients? Think visual identity, use of technology, types of services and products offered, and the age/demographic of both doctors and staff (maybe it's time to add some younger faces). Has your office fully adopted electronic medical records (EMR)? Do you have wireless internet available for patients in your waiting room? Do you use iPads in the office and provide them for waiting patients?

6.   Is your positioning losing relevance?

It wasn't long ago that offering eyeglasses in an hour was the leading edge of our market. Now, it's likely to be with high-tech lens products and treatments, edgy eyewear, and specialized medical services. Where are you in the minds of your patients and desired patients and how does your practice align with market trends? Are you ahead of the market, gaining relevance as the marketplace moves towards it? Don't lose relevance as your market powers ahead of you.

7. Are your touch points aligned with the market?

Still stocking an inventory of replacement contact lenses and solutions when you could take orders online and drop-ship from the manufacturer? Still spending money on mail promotions that get thrown away when you could be sending emails, text reminders, and electronic newsletters that patients actually read? Is your website up to date? Do you have a Facebook page and are you promoting it? You need to constantly align your patient touch points with their changing habits. Otherwise, your brand won't resonate with your market.

8. Is your entire patient experience in line with your desired brand?

Do you have photocopied brochures instead of custom color printed? Is that new instrument jammed into a closet that hasn't been designed for it? Have you yet to replace the stained ceiling tile in the waiting room? Everything must be aligned to speak to your brand.

9. Are you driving towards intimacy with your patients?

Do your patients know you and your staff as people? Or do you hide behind your white coat and ophthalmoscope? People want to do business with people — people they know and with whom they can relate. Do you connect with your patients in a meaningful, caring way? Not superficially, but with real, honest caring? Are you connected to your community? In today's high-tech society, being "high touch" is a sure point of differentiation.

10. Do you and your staff discuss your desired brand position?

At the heart of every successful brand and business is clarity. Don't leave your brand up to interpretation. Document your desired positioning and the why behind it. Discuss this frequently in staff meetings. Make the discussion a formal element of your new employee orientation process. Celebrate actions by staff that support your brand position.

Now ask yourself:

- How is my brand doing on each of these points? (Score your brand one through 10 in each area)
- How are my competitors doing on each of these points? (Score them, too)

At the end of the day, your best insulation from competition is to deliver a unique and valued patient experience. Make *you* very special and patients will know that they can't get *you* down the street.

CHAPTER 6

Managing Your Ego

Ego is the proverbial two-edged sword. Can't live with it, can't live without it. But if ever I've seen something get in the way of someone's success, myself included, it's the failure to understand and manage one's ego.

Ego is our inner voice — that voice in our head that speaks to us continually. It's our consciousness that most immediately controls our thoughts and behaviors and is most in touch with external reality.

Eckhart Tolle writes profoundly about ego in his book *A New Earth, Awakening to Your Life's Purpose.*[1] In his book, Mr. Tolle teaches us that vanity and pride are what most of us tend to think of when we think of ego, but ego is much more than an overinflated sense of self. It can also turn up in feelings of inferiority or self-hatred because ego is any image you have of yourself that gives you a sense of identity — and that identity derives from the things you tell yourself and the things other people have been saying about you that you've decided to accept as truth.

1 Eckhart Tolle, *A New Earth: Awakening to Your Life's Purpose* (New York: Plume, 2006).

Ego is a protective shell — like that of a turtle — and it serves as armor to cut you off from other people and the outside world. Ego brings about a sense of separation: "Here's me and there's the rest of the universe and other people." The ego likes to emphasize the otherness of others.

The ego loves to strengthen itself by complaining — either in thoughts or words — about other people, the situation you find yourself in, something that is happening right now but shouldn't be, and even about yourself. When this happens, the ego has you in its grip. You don't have thoughts; the thoughts have you. And if you want to be free, you have to understand that the voice in your head has created these thoughts, and the irritation and upset you feel is your emotional response to that voice. Only in this way can you be present to the truer world around you and see the golden shade in a pound of pears on the scanner or the delight of a child in line who begs to eat them. The trick, of course, is to work to free ourselves from this armor and from this voice that is dictating reality.

Ego is both good and evil. On the negative side, ego shuts us off from listening and learning. Ego drives us to make decisions that are not in the best interest of our whole. Ego causes us to react to stimuli in negative and sometimes very self-destructive ways. Ego gets us into trouble.

In group settings, I'm sure you've experienced a meeting participant who has something to say about everything. These individuals are inclined to share stories of their own success, rarely pausing to listen to the wisdom of others. They're often in one-up mode, needing to beat your story with theirs. Peel back the layers of these egocentric individuals and you'll often find trouble. Their egos won't allow them to seek help from others.

Have you ever walked into a team meeting and said to your team, "I don't know how to solve this problem?" Can you show your vulnerability to your employees, your friends, your family? I believe that the ability to be open about challenges, to trust those around you by being vulnerable, is the true test of whether one's ego is in the right place.

It's okay to have a strong ego; it's doubtful that one can be truly successful without it. But a leader must lead, and a manager must manage. To do so, I believe that it's equally important to show strength by showing that you need the help of others.

This concept is summarized for me in what's become known as the Stockdale Paradox.[2] James Stockdale (Ross Perot's vice presidential running mate) was the highest ranking prisoner of war (POW) during the Vietnam War. His seven-year captivity was particularly brutal; he was locked in leg irons inside the equivalent of a bath stall where he was severely tortured. To maintain a positive attitude towards his eventual release — and the release of his fellow POWs — Stockdale resolved:

"This is a very important lesson. You must never confuse faith that you will prevail in the end — which you can never afford to lose — with the discipline to confront the most brutal facts of your current reality, whatever they might be."[3]

---

2 James C. Collins, *Good to Great: Why Some Companies Make the Leap — and Others Don't* (New York: HarperBusiness, 2001).

3 Ibid.

Stockdale exuded confidence to his team that, eventually, they would be released. At the same time, he communicated the reality of their situation. It was that ability to balance resolve with reality that kept them alive. Keep your ego in its proper place and use it sparingly. You'll be a better leader — and a better person — for it.

CHAPTER 7

Defining and Creating Your Desired Culture

You've likely heard the term "clash of cultures" in the past. It's often used in business, usually in relation to the rationale for why a particular merger or acquisition wasn't as successful as was anticipated.

What I mean by culture in the context of this chapter is the behaviors and beliefs characteristic of your practice. Culture is different from brand, as brand exists on the outside while culture is decidedly internal. It is likely that culture creates brand. In most practices, culture simply evolves. And because culture is usually left up to chance, it often evolves negatively and unbeknownst even to the team that's living it. Defining and maintaining one's desired culture takes work and continuous monitoring, since culture evolves from your hiring and leadership practices. That said, I can't think of a more important exercise.

I personally experienced the negative side of this culture issue when I chose to relocate myself to the West Coast while leaving my small team in the East under the day-to-day direction of a couple of fledgling managers. While I returned to my operations center frequently, after about a year it became evident that I was seeing and experiencing a decline in teamwork. While I was on site, everything appeared rosy. But when I was gone, people did not get along as well, work seemed to drag, and stress was evident. I began to notice a general malaise — a below-the-surface unhappiness that was usurping my desired culture of collaboration and teamwork.

It was during a team retreat that I concluded that the problem was a lack of clarity in what I was seeking from my team in terms of culture. There appeared to have evolved a set of unwritten rules that were actually sabotaging our desired outcome. As a result, my team didn't know how to act in a variety of situations. What was evolving was a political organization, and I abhor politics.

I concluded that we all needed a very clear definition of our desired culture.

So, as a team, we set out on a journey. Our first step was to simply brainstorm the key words that we thought would describe our desired culture. From there, we chatted — again as a team — about how these words fit together and what they really meant to each of us. I then used this information to draft The Team Cleinman Culture, which I share as just one sample outcome of such a discovery process.

The Team Cleinman Culture

Cleinman Performance Partners is a successful, for-profit business enterprise that values the uniqueness and contributions of all its employees and associates.

At Cleinman Performance Partners, we employ and retain individuals who demonstrate the key attributes of intelligence, passion, attitude, respect, responsibility, and honesty.

In our interactions we seek first to understand, then to be understood. We will operate with transparency and communicate with candor. Unless there exists a viable, non-political reason for confidentiality, we can expect that our communications will be shared and will speak and write about others accordingly.

Because we view mistakes as learning experiences, we promote an environment that fosters creativity, entrepreneurship, and risk taking. We see different opinions and views as opportunities to learn and grow. We will cherish and nurture the ideas of others as if they were our own.

We place issues in their proper perspective and focus our corrective actions on improving our systems, not on blame. We constantly seek to identify and nurture the strengths of everyone on our team and to draw on those strengths in our planning and decision making.

The respect we show for each other also extends to our clients, vendors, and everyone with whom we interact.

As unique, creative associates in a vibrant business, we will honor and protect each other. We recognize it is our individual and collective responsibility to hold one another accountable for living our culture. It is our individual responsibility to help those who may, from time to time, stray from the culture we share and value.

We honor and reward each other when we live our culture.

And we have fun as we face each day's challenges and possibilities.

What's critically important is not the outcome but the process. The entire team was involved in this exploration. My charge to the team was that there were no sacred cows; that everything and anything should be considered. We worked together on the effort over a six-month period.

Once our culture statement was reasonably finalized (we review it at least annually as a team), it became evident that ours was a great set of words. But something was missing. How would we go about attaining our desired culture? This took some further exploration — both from a leadership perspective as well as at the team level. The result was a clear set of rules that, if followed judiciously, would result in our desired culture:

The Rules by Which We Live The Team Cleinman Culture

- It is everyone's responsibility to be the role model for our culture.

- It is everyone's responsibility to give each other the benefit of the doubt and to depersonalize issues and questions.

- It is everyone's responsibility to be direct with each other and to communicate with candor.

- It is everyone's responsibility to be open to such direct communication and to see such communication as constructive.

- It is everyone's responsibility to have patience and to deal with each other professionally and equitably.

- It is everyone's responsibility to stop personal attacks and politics in their tracks.

- It is everyone's responsibility to ask questions, to provide background to those questions, and to expect answers.

- It is everyone's responsibility to communicate and help each other understand:
    - What is the nature of our relationship?
    - What do you expect of me? I of you?
    - How will we deal with authority?
    - How will we handle and resolve conflict?

- It is everyone's responsibility to understand the appropriate forums for communicating and resolving issues — and to use them.

- It is everyone's responsibility to help each other with these ideals.

- It is everyone's responsibility to hold each other accountable to these ideals.

The Team Cleinman culture statement isn't a static document that is relegated to the files. It's posted throughout our building, shared with every prospective employee, and is an integral part of each team member's work contract. We review our culture statement with the entire team on an annual basis and discuss any cultural issues as they arise. This has become an important touchstone for our team and is referred to often.

I encourage you to explore the question: What is my desired culture?

Of importance to mention here is that this process is just like any other goal-setting process. With our culture statement, we laid out a goal. But it became clear to us all during the exercise that a goal without a clear set of actions to accomplish it is relatively worthless. Thus, regardless of your goal (e.g., winning a football game), you must define the means to that end (let's score 3.4 yards on every down). Without the means, you can't attain the goal. And, to ensure that you have a chance at achieving your goal, your team must participate in the process.

> *"Tell me and I'll forget; show me and I may remember; involve me and I'll understand."*[1]
>
> — *Chinese Proverb*

Lastly, recognize that culture evolves, and what worked yesterday may no longer be appropriate today. As I finish this book, we are in the midst of re-engineering our culture statement. Our desire is to retain the original value while simplifying the communication.

---

1 "Tell Me and I'll Forget; Show Me and I May Remember; Involve Me and I'll Understand," *Search Quotes.* http://www.searchquotes.com/quotation/Tell_me_and_I'll_forget;_show_me_and_I_may_remember;_involve_me_and_I'll_understand./240987/.

CHAPTER 8

Delegate

Dr. Jane grosses over $1 million per year with an outstanding net. She's dynamic and her patients love her. She has a beautiful facility which she designed herself. She toils late into the evening handling coding and billing issues, paying her bills, designing forms and promotions, and reviewing products. As her practice has grown, so, too, has her workload. She experiences continual staff turn-over, exacerbating her stress. She's often heard saying "I just can't find good help." She's turned down opportunities to be involved in her community and she misses her daughter's soccer games.

Dr. Jane recognizes that her primary responsibility is to provide solutions for her patients. She does a good job at it; she's got a great education and has honed her medical skills for the past decade. She's smart and she knows it. But something's wrong. While successful on the outside, Dr. Jane has turned into a miserable workaholic. And now it's impacting both her practice and her personal life.

Dr. Jane has failed to distinguish between her role as a doctor and her role as a CEO.

Chapter 8: Delegate

Dr. Jane thinks like a doctor regardless of the hat that she's wearing. As a result, she micro-manages her team, providing them with detailed direction as it relates not only to desired outcomes, but to the individual steps necessary for project completion as well. Then Dr. Jane hovers over the work. Jane is a perfectionist and expects perfection with every task. Thus, Dr. Jane, who does attempt to hire good people, burns them out by failing to allow them to develop their skills. Her motto is "It's easier to do it myself."

Many years ago, I found myself in Dr. Jane's shoes. I remember speaking to an acquaintance of mine, the retired CEO of a Fortune 500 company. I was lamenting about how I couldn't seem to get my then small staff to do things the way that I wanted them done. At the time — and I remember it well — I was actually reviewing a letter to a vendor, drafted by my bookkeeper, about a mistake on a recent invoice. Like everything else I was trying to do, the letter had to be perfect and I found myself investing 30 minutes on what I later concluded was a ridiculous waste of my time. My friend's response to my query: "Most of the time, 85 percent is just fine." In other words, most of the time, imperfection is okay. It's that extra 15 percent that saps the strength of an enterprise.

Now, I'm not implying that you can have imperfection and be successful. What my friend was actually saying was, "allow your team to fail." It's only through failure that we learn. And if, as leaders, we are too quick to take on projects ourselves, we end up with the precise opposite effect of what we desire. We end up enabling the very mediocrity that we wish to avoid, since our team develops a learned response to our requests — namely: "Don't work too hard on the project, since he'll just change it, correct it, and criticize it."

Several times a year, I come across this problem in a variety of ways. I remember visiting a practice for a review and, opening the bathroom door, I found the door knob very loose and wobbly. I asked the senior staff member how long the door handle had been loose, to which she replied, "About six months. We keep asking Doc to fix the problem, but he hasn't gotten to it."

There are certainly tasks and projects that require your involvement, but, in reality, if you've laid out a clear vision for your desired outcomes, you can delegate most tasks. Further, if you provide your team with effective leadership and permission, things like door handles get fixed without your even knowing there was a problem.

The tool that I encourage my clients to use to help their delegation process is to take a deck of index cards and list, one per card, each of the tasks that you do. Over a two-week period, simply write these cards out as you handle or think of each of the tasks.

For instance:
- Write referral letters to physicians
- Review medical coding of each chart
- Call patients
- Pay bills

After two weeks, sort through your cards and remove any duplicates. Then rank the cards from tasks you perform that are least important to those that are most important. Now, every Monday morning, take one or two of the cards and get rid of them. "Mary, from now on I'd like you to handle writing checks to vendors. Let's work together over the next month so I can share with you how I handle things and then this will become your responsibility." Delegate the work, but don't abdicate. Stay involved until you're confident that the task is being properly performed and the individual to whom you've delegated it clearly understands not just what to do but also why it's being done. When people understand the why of things, they can figure out the how of things even in changing circumstances.

You'll be amazed at what you can get rid of. Further, your team will become more self-sufficient, more enthusiastic, and more satisfied when they have been delegated both the responsibility of the job and the authority necessary to get the job done. And lastly, your practice will benefit from the additional time that you now have to focus on more strategic, bigger-picture issues.

> *Surround yourself with good people, nurture them, and get out of their way. Let their success be yours.*

CHAPTER 9

Decisions, Decisions, Decisions

In previous chapters, we discussed the importance of delegation and the role of the CEO as an individual who asks questions and makes decisions. We spoke about the conflict between your role as a medical professional and your role as CEO. The two roles come together in the decision-making process. At the end of the day, whether wearing your optometrist hat or your CEO hat, the reality is that you're a decision maker.

Think about your daily routine. A patient comes in for her 8:30 a.m. appointment. During her 20 minutes with you, you review her history, ask a few probing questions, successfully diagnose the problem, and set a course of treatment. Finally, you establish a follow-up plan and actions. You do so without hesitancy. Take a moment to review and write down the medical decisions that you made just today. Now do the same for the business side. I think you'll find a large difference.

Certainly, you make a lot of medical decisions, and the volume of your medical decision making will likely outweigh that of your business decisions. But my point here is the ease with which you make these decisions and the process that you use. You make medical decisions with rapidity because you trust your medical education and experience. You make medical decisions with ease because you have a system for doing so.

As it relates to business decisions, you are likely very slow and somewhat haphazard in the process because:

1. business decisions require analysis and input that you generally leave on your shoulders;

2. you lack confidence and experience in this area;

3. as a result, you don't trust yourself.

Another difference between your medical decision making and your business decision making is that an error with the former is much, much more problematic than an error on the latter. Does this make sense? We make critical decisions involving the health and well-being of our patients in warp speed and yet we agonize over what color the waiting room should be painted or whether Mary should receive a raise.

In his ground-breaking book *Blink: The Power of Thinking without Thinking*, author Malcolm Gladwell takes a scientific approach to understanding how we make decisions; about how we think about thinking. He explores why some decisions appear to come so easily while others are painful — how some people seem to make brilliant decisions in the blink of an eye while others are consistently inept. At the end of the day, Malcolm says, go with your gut. Because your instincts are the sum total of all of your life's learning.[1]

Isn't that how your medical decision making works? Generally, you go with your gut. Because, after 10,000 patients, you've likely seen most of what you're ever going to see. You have the experience and you have the process.

Likewise it is with business decision making. It's really the same process as that of your medical decisions. You gather information, form a diagnosis, lay out a treatment plan and follow up. What's interesting about business decisions is that they're rarely life or death, and one most often learns something from failure — sometimes even more so than from success.

In my own world, I tend to make decisions rapidly and encourage my team members to do the same. Further, I abhor endless analysis, as it saps the strength of an organization and a team. Better to make a bad decision than no decision.

In his book *The Decision Maker,* author Dennis Bakke lays forth the means by which leaders can dramatically relieve themselves of decisions. His approach is to delegate decisions in much the same way as one delegates tasks. Mr. Bakke defines a method to ensure that more gets accomplished with less stress by assigning the actual decision to a team member.[2] His is a refreshing approach and you'll find his book a useful tool.

When you build an empowered team — one which is comprised of smart people to whom you effectively delegate

---

1 Malcolm Gladwell, *Blink: The Power of Thinking without Thinking* (New York: Little, Brown and Company, 2005).

2 Dennis Bakke, *The Decision Maker* (Seattle: Pear Press, 2003).

— they will do much of your diagnosis and analysis for you. With an empowered team, they will present you with possible solutions, and you should encourage this. As a result, armed with their analysis and recommendations and your well-defined values and brand, you can make final decisions rapidly and with confidence.

> *Destroy bureaucracy. See clearly the decisions that are yours. Make them!*

CHAPTER 10

Get the Right People in the Right Seats

Sally has been with the practice for 10 years. Some days she's a great producer, but, more often than not, she's just not operating on all cylinders. Sally is an underperformer, but you just can't bring yourself to let her go. One of the reasons that the decision is tearing you up is that you remember Sally when you first hired her as your bookkeeper. Sally did an outstanding job in that role for five years. She was so good, and learned so fast that, when your optician left, you promoted Sally into that spot. After all, Sally did an outstanding job and you needed an optician. So what happened?

Sally may be a good employee, but you promoted her to failure. She may be the right person for your team, but she's in the wrong seat. This situation is very common, and what's interesting is that it can be largely avoided. Your job as CEO is to ensure that the people you and your team hire are right for the practice and right for the specific job.

In his amazing study of successful companies in the book *Good to Great: Why Some Companies Make the Leap—and Others Don't*, author Jim Collins identified 13 companies that reached the pinnacle of performance. He discussed how these firms moved from good to great by ensuring that they had "the right people on the bus and the wrong people off the bus." Mr. Collins' premise is that good teams can accomplish most anything and that a CEO's first responsibility is to ensure that he or she has the right team in place; that this is more important than even having a winning business plan or strategy.[1]

So, I ask you, do you look at your team as an expense or as an asset? It's clear from our work that, more often than not, peak performance in optometry practices can be traced directly to the leader's underlying attitude towards the team. Underperformers often think of staff as expendable; they should be paid as little as possible and be driven as hard as possible. They look at labor costs with a short-term, critical eye.

Top performers clearly see their team as an asset. They work hard at making careful selections. They invest in team and individual development. Top performers use a variety of tools, including detailed position descriptions, defined interview questions, multiple interviews, behavior and psychological assessments, and professional background checks. They invest to ensure that they have the best chance at success with a new hire. They clearly focus on having the right people in the right job.

Back to Sally, the optician. The root problem is that Sally exhibits the behaviors that make for a successful bookkeeper. Sally is very detail oriented, rather slow to act (because of her conscientiousness), and tends to be more of an introvert,

---

1 Collins, *Good to Great*.

although she's a pretty good actor. Her natural behaviors are in conflict with those behaviors normally demonstrated by successful opticians. The optician job requires a true love of people and the ability to juggle many different situations without stress. In some respects, the bookkeeper's job and the optician's job require behaviors that are polar opposite. Sally's performance challenges are directly related to her flexing her natural tendencies too greatly, resulting in stress. It is this underlying stress that is the root cause of Sally's less-than-stellar performance.

Behavior Profiling Primer[2]

Certain positions require a certain set of behaviors. We learn about these behaviors by understanding what is commonly referred to as DISC, the four-quadrant behavioral model based on the work of William Moulton Marston Ph.D. (1893 – 1947). DISC examines the behavior of individuals in their environment or within a specific situation. DISC therefore focuses on the styles and preferences of such behavior. The father of DISC graduated from doctoral studies at Harvard in the newly developing field of psychology and was also a consulting psychologist, researcher, and author or co-author of five books.

The DISC system provides dimensions of communication and has become known as the universal language of behavior. Research has found that characteristics of behavior can be

---

2 Copyrighted material courtesy of Target Training International, Ltd.

grouped into four major styles and they tend to exhibit specific characteristics common to that particular style. All individuals possess all four, but what differs from one to another is the extent of each.

For most, these types are seen in shades of gray rather than black or white, and within that, there is interplay of behaviors, otherwise known as blends. The denotation of such blends would be starting with the primary (or stronger) type, followed by the secondary (or lesser) type, although all contribute more than just purely the strength of that signal.

Having understood the differences between these blends makes it possible to integrate individual team members with less troubleshooting, i.e., knowing where to remedy is no longer the issue, although it still takes dedication on everyone's part not to step on one another's toes.

Having said that, there are varying degrees of compatibility, not just toward tasks, but interpersonal relationships as well. However, when they are identified, energy can be directed toward refining the results.

Each of these types has its own unique value to the team, ideal environment, general characteristics, what the individual is motivated by and value to team.

DISC is also used in an assortment of areas and used by many companies, HR professionals, organizations, consultants, trainers — the list goes on, due to its host of benefits.

Method

The assessments classify four aspects of behavior by testing a person's preferences in word associations. DISC is an acronym for:

- **Dominance** — relating to control, power and assertiveness

- **Influence** — relating to social situations and communication

- **Steadiness** (submission in Marston's time) — relating to patience, persistence, and thoughtfulness

- **Conscientiousness** (or caution, compliance in Marston's time) — relating to structure and organization

These four dimensions can be grouped in a grid with D and I sharing the top row and representing extroverted aspects of the personality, and C and S below representing introverted aspects. D and C then share the left column and represent task-focused aspects, and I and S share the right column and represent social aspects. In this matrix, the vertical dimension represents a factor of Assertive or Passive, while the horizontal represents Open versus Guarded.

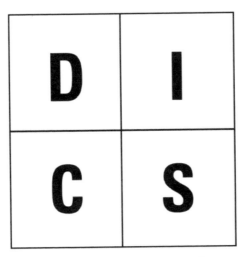

Dominance: People who score high in the intensity of the "D" styles factor are very active in dealing with problems and challenges, while low "D" scores are people who want to do more research before committing to a decision. High "D" people are described as demanding, forceful, egocentric, strong willed, driving, determined, ambitious, aggressive, and pioneering. Low "D" scores describe those who are conservative, low keyed, cooperative, calculating, undemanding, cautious, mild, agreeable, modest and peaceful.

Influence: People with High "I" scores influence others through talking and activity and tend to be emotional. They are described as convincing, magnetic, political, enthusiastic, persuasive, warm, demonstrative, trusting, and optimistic. Those with Low "I" scores influence more by data and facts, and not with feelings. They are described as reflective, factual, calculating, skeptical, logical, suspicious, matter of fact, pessimistic, and critical.

Steadiness: People with High "S" styles scores want a steady pace, security, and do not like sudden change. High "S" persons are calm, relaxed, patient, possessive, predictable, deliberate, stable, consistent, and tend to be unemotional and poker faced. Low "S" intensity scores are those who like change and variety. People with Low "S" scores are described as restless, demonstrative, impatient, eager, or even impulsive.

Conscientious: Persons with High "C" styles adhere to rules, regulations, and structure. They like to do quality work and do it right the first time. High "C" people are careful, cautious, exacting, neat, systematic, diplomatic, accurate, and tactful. Those with Low "C" scores challenge the rules and want independence and are described as self-willed, stubborn, opinionated, unsystematic, arbitrary, and careless with details.

Each of these attributes is present in all of us. As a leader, your job is to understand the appropriate combination of behaviors for each position and to ensure that your team has a good understanding of these behaviors, as this will greatly assist them in dealing with different types of patients.

For additional information on behavior profiles and how to use them within your practice, visit our website at www.cleinman.com/consulting/human-resources.

CHAPTER 11

It's All About Systems

It's likely that, sometime in the past few months, you've jumped on an airplane to head to some far-off destination. Leading your trip were two individuals — the pilot (you) and the copilot (your office manager) together with a well-trained crew of flight attendants (your staff). Larry, the pilot, has been flying commercial jets for over 30 years. He's logged over 25,000 hours doing so. He knows his stuff.

What's the first thing Larry does when he steps into the cockpit? In spite of all of his years of experience, Larry pulls out the checklist of sequential actions necessary to get the plane off the ground. He follows that checklist, item by item, as he starts up the engines. You can even hear him communicating with his co-pilot. "Oil pressure light green?" he asks. "Check," is the response.

Dr. Tom is frustrated. Sarah, his receptionist, called in sick this morning (again). While this results in a host of problems for the small team, the most challenging issue is that it's Sarah's responsibility to handle the office telephone system. Tomorrow is a holiday, and no one besides Sarah seems to know how to put the special announcement on the messaging system. There's no documentation to be found anywhere. Sarah can't be reached. So, Dr. Tom spends his lunch hour figuring out how to save the day. This kind of thing seems to occur frequently.

> *"People don't run businesses. Systems run businesses. People run systems."*[1]

If there's one word that can free you and your organization from a world of chaos and emotional reactions, it's "systems." Now, you likely already have them. You have a method for answering the phone, for sending recall notices, for entering charges, etc. But it is also likely that these systems are not well documented and, worse, the team doesn't look at them as systems. Each is left to his or her own methodologies for getting things accomplished. Each staff member keeps these methods locked away in their brain, feeling a sense of security from being the one person on the team who knows how to perform a particular task.

Contrast this with the practice that has every system documented on the office computer network, carefully outlined and keyword searchable. This "how we do things here" tool is available for any staff member to view. It's reviewed and updated by the individual leading the task on a quarterly basis.

---

1 Gerber, *The E-myth Revisited.*

Each weekly staff meeting includes a 15-minute review of an individual system on a rotating basis. The entire team has input into the steps and processes. Further, the team continually reviews whether each step is actually necessary or is a duplicate of some other step in some other process. This is a team with ownership — a high-performing organization.

Systems — and "system think" — are key to developing a high-performing organization. Systems are step-by-step methodologies for accomplishing a desired task. They are best defined and managed by the people actually doing the work. They don't have to be complex, but should be understandable to anyone on the team. And they should be living and breathing, frequently reviewed, and adjusted as needed (think continuous improvement).

For one thing, focusing on the system takes our focus off people. Yes, people make mistakes, and having people make mistakes is frustrating. But, more often than not, mistakes occur because of a system breakdown. When we focus our attention on discovering and plugging the holes in systems, we depersonalize the problem. As a result, our teams get focused on doing the right things in the right way at the right time with the right results.

Example of a System

The Cleinman Performance Partners' Recruiting Process

Project Start
- Need established & approved
- Service order submitted

Advertising
- Advertising service order submitted
- Advertising venues agreed upon
- Advertising placed

Candidates
- Applicants reviewed — qualified applicants sent to hiring manager
- Phone screens completed
- Onsite interviews scheduled
- Assessments & "homework" (books to read, etc.) completed

Due Diligence
- Background check
- Credit report
- References checked

Offer
- Offer extended by hiring manager / Offer accepted by candidate
- Agreements signed by candidate
- Start date established

Communications
- Other candidates notified position has been filled
- Staff notified of the hire

Onboarding
- Proceed to onboarding process

CHAPTER 12

Creating a Culture of Continuous Improvement

Back in the mid 1980s, I had the good fortune to visit 3M's headquarters in St. Paul, Minnesota. Sitting in the reception area awaiting the start of my meeting, I noticed a large sign displaying the venerable firm's mission statement. While the totality of the statement is lost in my memory, I'll never forget this part: "25% of our annual business will result from products that were not in existence five years ago."

That message, to me, was an epiphany. 3M, after all, is a huge company. How could such a mega-organization commit to such a lofty goal? Sure, 3M is world renowned for their product development. Everyone's heard the story about the glue that was designated useless, as it wouldn't firmly attach to anything. That glue became Post-It Notes and an entire brand of products. Often, innovation is about never giving up — about uncovering a breakthrough from something that didn't work for its intended purpose. 3M's innovation list is a mile long (including our industry's LEAP blocking system). How do they do it?

A Different Perspective

I decided to try to understand 3M's innovation system. With a little research, I didn't find a system, but discovered that innovation is the very foundation of the firm's entire culture. You see, a guy by the name of William McKnight joined Minnesota Mining and Manufacturing Company in 1907 as an assistant bookkeeper. He quickly rose through the company, became president in 1929 and chairman of the board in 1949. He retired in 1966 after 59 years with the firm. Many believe McKnight's greatest contribution was as a business philosopher, since he created the corporate culture of which we're speaking — one that encourages employee initiative and innovation. In 1948, McKnight is believed to have laid out his basic management philosophy:

"As our business grows, it becomes increasingly necessary to delegate responsibility and to encourage men and women to exercise their initiative. This requires considerable tolerance. Those men and women, to whom we delegate authority and responsibility, if they are good people, are going to want to do their jobs in their own way... Mistakes will be made. But... Management that is destructively critical when mistakes are made kills initiative. And it's essential that we have many people with initiative if we are to continue to grow."[1]

What I interpret Mr. McKnight to have accomplished was to take a strategic approach to the development of his people

1 Robert Roepke, Ritu Agarwal, and Thomas W. Ferratt, "Aligning the IT Human Resource with Business Vision: The Leadership Initiative at 3M," *MIS Quarterly*, Vol. 24, no. 2 (June, 2000): 329 (accessed June 3, 2015), doi: 10.2307/3250941.

and create the foundation for a culture of innovation and continuous change. He recognized that investing in people and their mistakes builds an innovative and confident enterprise.

So, what happens in your practice when someone takes initiative? By its very nature, initiative requires making mistakes. Do you celebrate mistakes or do you and your team beat new ideas and improvement suggestions back in a variety of overt and covert ways? Do you find yourself injecting wisdom so as to avoid mistakes by your team? Do you have a culture of "Tried it — didn't work?"

Creating a culture of continuous improvement requires significant open-mindedness and objectivity. Most of the individuals on your team are likely high on the steadiness scale (see Chapter 10), which means they are less likely to enjoy a fast-paced, highly changing organization. For these individuals, if you're not careful, they can see the desire for change to be a criticism of their work. Organizationally, you must separate the two. Asking your team to look at everything they do with an ongoing eye for improvement is distinctly different than criticizing what's been done to date. The analogy that I extend is that your team is that of a child just learning to walk. You can see it in your mind's eye: a little girl crawls over to the edge of the chair, reaches up with tiny arms, grabs the edge of the chair with an iron-like grip and pulls herself up on wobbly legs for the first effort at standing. She staggers for a moment then — *plop* — she topples over. And what do you say when we see this happening?

A Different Perspective

You say, "Atta girl! Way to go!" and other forms of endearing and personal encouragement. You don't say, "You know, if you'd done it this way, you would've been able to stand."

Encouraging self-confidence by allowing and celebrating mistakes is a critical component of organizational and personal development. Without mistakes, the team can't learn success. And, if you're there at every turn attempting to prevent mistakes, you'll never develop an innovative and learned team.

CHAPTER 13

Creating a Culture of Ownership

You live in a nice home that you keep well maintained. Your lawn is well manicured. Each weekend, you make it a point to get your car washed. You're diligent in making sure that you have your car's oil changed every 3,000 miles. You drive your nice car to the airport, parking carefully to ensure as best you can that your car isn't smacked by the door of the vehicle beside yours.

You jump on a plane and arrive at your destination, where you rent a car and check into a hotel room. If you're like most travelers, when you departed your skybus, you left gum wrappers in the seat pockets together with your used newspapers. When you left your hotel room each morning, your bed was unmade, there were wet towels strewn about, and dirty laundry was heaped in a corner. The cleaners at the rental car company experienced a backseat floor littered with the accumulated trash of your three-day excursion.

What's the difference? Simply stated, it's the disparity between owning and renting. Consciously or unconsciously, as a renter, you're aware that cleaning up the mess is someone else's responsibility.

The same is the case in business. Do you find yourself feeling that you care more about the office environment than do your employees? It is every leader's primary responsibility to get the team to assume ownership, whether directly or indirectly.

In his amazing book *The Great Game of Business*, Jack Stack tells the true story of Springfield Remanufacturing Company (SRC) — then a division of International Harvester — which was in serious trouble. It was, in fact, on the verge of closure. Jack tells how he and his small group of managers pulled together $100,000 and took on $9 million in debt to acquire this floundering business and save the 150 jobs that went with it.[1] In a relatively short period of time, Jack and his team turned this failure of a plant into a money machine. Today, some 30 years later, SRC is actually a group of more than 17 companies. A share in SRC that was originally worth 10 cents was worth $361 in 2012. The firm moved from $16 million in sales in 1983 to more than $450 million in 2012.[2]

What was Jack's secret? Make everyone an owner; the vast majority of SRC employees are actual shareholders in the company. Jack opened the business world's eyes to the concept of employee ownership.

Now, in most states, it isn't legal to have employees be direct owners of a professional practice. But effectively using the

---

1 Jack Stack and Bo Burlingham. *The Great Game of Business* (New York: Currency Doubleday, 1994).

2 Vera L. Street, Marc D. Street, Christy H. Weer, and Frank Shipper, "SRC Holdings: Winning The Game While Sharing The Prize," *Journal of Business Case Studies*, Vol. 10, no. 1 (First Quarter, 2014): 43-58.

principals of ownership can make a dramatic difference in the performance of your practice. One of those guiding principles is open-book management.

Imagine playing football without keeping score. At the end of the day, your team knows that they're tired, sweaty, dirty and achy. What they don't know is what they've accomplished. Practices that fail to share information about performance are like that football team. There's no clear understanding of purpose because the purpose is largely intangible. There's no score, no "stake in the outcome."[3]

To show you how powerful it is to keep score, create the following chart and post it in an area visible to all employees (break area or lab):

Post Average Sale Daily

	Optician 1	Optician 2	Optician 3
Mon			
Tues			
Wed			
Thurs			
Fri			
Sat			

Average Sale = (Frame Revenue + Lens Revenue) ÷ Pairs of Lenses Sold

---

3 Jack Stack and Bo Burlingham, *A Stake in the Outcome: Building a Culture of Ownership for the Long-term Success of Your Business* (New York: Currency, 2002).

Now, ask that your opticians simply calculate their average sale and post it daily. Let them do the work. Here's the likely result:

Post Average Sale Daily

	Optician 1	Optician 2	Optician 3
Mon	$249	$278	$302
Tues	$248	$281	$299
Wed	$265	$302	$321
Thurs	$271	$314	$324
Fri	$281	$326	$319
Sat	$279	$315	$322

Average Sale = (Frame Revenue + Lens Revenue) ÷ Pairs of Lenses Sold

As I'm confident you will experience, making team members aware of performance through an objective measurement (note: you're not measuring total sales, simply average sale) exposes them to their score and, as a result, natural competition sets in and performance improves. What you do want to avoid is negative competitiveness that can manifest itself in catty behavior, patient grabbing, etc. When and if such behavior arises, you must deal with it directly. Not everyone on the team can be the top scorer, but everyone can celebrate the top-scoring individual and learn from them.

This is but one small example of open-book management, the technique used by Jack Stack to transform all his team members into owners. The technique provides everyone on the team with all relevant financial information about the practice, including revenue, profit, cost of goods, cash flow, and expenses. The goal is to provide information so team members can make better decisions, resulting in much greater understanding of what actions are needed to meet the goals of the enterprise and dramatically improve teamwork.

The basic rules for open-book management are to give employees:

- training to understand the financial information;
- all relevant financial information;
- responsibility for the numbers under their control; and
- a financial stake in how the company performs.

Successful open-book practices ensure every team member at all levels is fully knowledgeable about how their job fits into the financial plan of the practice. However, taking a practice from its historical mode of closed book to open book is not as easy as just starting training classes on financial performance. Employees (and, let's face it, optometrists) rarely find it compelling to understand all of the numbers. Typically, to overcome this problem, open-book management focuses us on a specific critical number. Your critical number should be a rather simple unit of measurement that leads to the desired outcome.

The critical number will likely be different for every practice and can be different from year to year. Here are some critical numbers for optometry practices:

- New patient volume
- Revenue per OD hour
- Total number of exams
- Revenue per exam
- Cost of goods
- Payroll costs per patient
- Managed care write-offs

The numbers can be different for every practice, but it should be a number that represents a prime indicator of profitability or a specific, overriding goal for the year. Discovering this critical number is a key component of creating an open-book practice. Once discovered, a scoreboard is then developed to bring together all the numbers needed to calculate the critical number. The scoreboard is open for all to see, and meetings take place to discuss how individuals can influence the direction of the score and, therefore, the direction of the critical number. Finally, a stake in the outcome is provided which can be a bonus plan (see Chapter 14) that is tied to critical number performance.

Ownership is the key to developing a truly high-performing practice that operates successfully in your absence, retains high-performing employees, and delivers exceptional patient care day in and day out. The keys to ownership are information and a stake in the outcome.

That which is measured improves.

CHAPTER 14

Incentivizing the Team

You cannot hope to develop a culture of ownership without providing a direct connection between results and rewards. This is most often accomplished in the form of an incentive plan. There are scores of ways to incentivize your team, but there are some rules of the road that should be followed carefully.

What Every Incentive Program Needs

- **A clear performance-outcome relationship.** Explicitly set out performance levels to be rewarded as well as the value of the reward at each performance level.

- **Employee control over the performance to be rewarded.** Eliminate factors outside employees' control (scheduling, inventory deficiencies, equipment failure) that could defeat their efforts to reach the performance level.

- **A valued incentive.** If it is to act as a motivator of behavior, an incentive must be valued by the employee.

Also, award the incentive soon after it has been earned to strengthen the performance-outcome relationship.

Creating an effective incentive plan is not rocket science. However, it does require you to roll up your sleeves and do a bit of research, ask some probing questions, and make some decisions.

First, ask yourself what you want the outcome of the incentive plan to be, how you expect to achieve this outcome, and who should be involved in making it happen. After you decide these three things, you will have a good idea of the particular type of plan your practice needs.

The What

Suppose Dr. Jim believes that revenue (and, as a result, profits) are not where they should be. He could offer an incentive based simply on increased revenue, but this goal is just not specific enough. Increased revenue is the result of specific actions.

For example, it doesn't address why revenues aren't higher. Is it the product? The optician's approach? Lack of customer service? Is it Dr. Jim's difficulty in consistently handing off the patient to the opticians or a lack of training? There are many factors that can impact revenue.

In addition, Dr. Jim has no idea how much growth he should expect to award. What's his goal?

Now, let's say Dr. Jim, as a member of the Cleinman Performance Network, is aware that average revenue per exam* averages $404 in practices of his type while his practice only produces $300. That difference spells opportunity and gives him and his team an idea of where some changes need to occur.

At this point, together with his team, he decides that increasing revenue per exam is the measurable outcome that he wants from his incentive plan. This becomes his critical number for the coming year towards which the entire team is directed.

The How

Now, Dr. Jim needs to figure out how to make this happen. Dr. Jim could decide unilaterally that the staff could accomplish the 30 percent increase required to meet the goal simply by working harder. But a more intelligent choice is to motivate the staff to work smarter by involving them in changing the entire team's methods (including Dr. Jim), focusing their efforts, or both.

Dr. Jim explains the situation to his team. He reviews the benchmarks and engages his team in a discussion that leads them to arrive at the same conclusion that he has — that a 30 percent increase in revenue per exam is achievable. However, during the discussion, Dr. Jim must be open to other ideas and have a willingness to modify his goal based upon team input. Without this buy-in from the team, it is unlikely the goal will be achieved. Based on the discussion, Dr. Jim announces a 30

* Collected revenue per comprehensive exam

percent increase in revenue per exam as an objective for the practice for the coming year and his plan to directly share part of that increase with the staff. He points out that other practices of his type are typically realizing 30 percent higher revenue per exam and asks the staff to brainstorm ways they could increase this critical number.

Ideas begin to emerge; some are more practical than others. As a group, Dr. Jim and his staff set the following specific actions to achieve the goal:

- The front desk will encourage patients to bring all their eyewear with them when they come for an exam. This provides the doctor and opticians with an opportunity to review all the patients' Rxs and to make recommendations accordingly. Of course, the front desk will encourage all patients to make appointments for family members at the same time to ensure that the appointment book is 95 percent full each week.

- The practice will hire an additional optician to bring their staff hours per exam up to the target level. They recognize that the Achilles heel of selling is ensuring that there's enough time with the patient.

- The doctor and clinical staff will encourage all contact lens wearers to acquire plano or Rx sunglasses. The numerical goal will be to increase sunwear sales by 20 percent and, indeed, they'll accomplish this by packaging contact lens purchases with sunwear sales.

- The optical staff will upgrade the eyewear selection to increase the average price of frames displayed by $25 by adding higher-end eyewear and adjusting price points. Their target is to increase the sale of premium lenses from 25 percent of sales to 50 percent.

- The opticians will package their lens offerings (good, better, best) and target an increase in AR lenses from the current 30 percent to 75 percent.

- Dr. Jim will begin writing a minimum of two Rxs for each patient (street, occupational, sport, sunwear) to teach patients that different lenses are required for different uses.

- The practice will install a paging system so that Dr. Jim can call opticians back to the exam lane to effectively hand off the patient to the optician within the doctor environment.

- All patients, regardless of whether they have an Rx change, will be seated in optical for a tuneup of their eyewear. This provides the optician with an opportunity to engage in dialogue about new products.

Now, Dr. Jim and the team have developed a specific, measurable objective for the incentive plan that employees can understand. They all have clear strategies with measurable goals to use in reaching the objective. All members of the team are part of attaining the critical number.

The Who

The "who" refers to which employees will participate in the incentive plan and on what basis. Incentives that are paid to individuals assume that work is performed independently and that one individual alone is responsible for the outcome. We all know this is rarely the case in an eye care practice. It's much more advisable to reward the entire team for working together effectively to reach a common goal.

The How Much

Dr. Jim has ascertained that a 30 percent increase in his revenue per exam will yield a $250,000 increase in revenue and drive a $100,000 increase in net profit. Dr. Jim is willing to share 25 percent of that gain, so Dr. Jim has devised this incentive plan:

Goal	Incentive Pool
10% increase in $$/exam	$5,000
15%	$7,500
20%	$10,000
25%	$15,000
30%	$25,000
35%	$35,000

Because collections per exam can be calculated daily, Dr. Jim had the team post a big chart in the staff lounge. The chart shows daily graphs and a thermometer displaying their monthly progress towards their goal. The incentive pool is an annualized bonus that is paid quarterly and split among the team based upon hours worked. As the bonus and goal are for annual performance, the incentive pool pays out 10 percent in the first quarter, 20 percent in the second, 30 percent in the third, and 40 percent in the fourth. This prevents an overpayment of the bonus pool early on in the event of a performance decline. The team met weekly for 15 minutes to review progress and brainstorm additional ideas about how to move the number.

As a result, Dr. Jim and his team were all fully engaged in the improvement plan, and they met their 30 percent goal.

CHAPTER 15

Delivering the WOW!

What is it that you sell? Are you providing preventive eye health care? Are you providing patients with improved vision? Are you providing fashion eyewear? Certainly, if you're like most optometrists, you're looking to deliver all of the above. But, in reality, that's what everyone strives to provide. Delivering those things is not what will develop patient loyalty and the resulting referrals that are the key to practice growth.

Dr. Mary is a vivacious and driven professional practicing in an upscale community on the outskirts of a major city. She and her team continually go out of their way to provide exceptional service. Everywhere she goes, Dr. Mary makes it a point to talk about her profession. Everyone is her friend.

At the beginning of what was expected to be a particularly busy day, Dr. Mary was called into the practice earlier than usual to assist a new patient with a dry eye concern. The patient never showed. Late that afternoon, the patient showed up at the office hoping to see Dr. Mary. Dr. Mary agreed to see the patient, fitting him in at the end of her busy day.

Chapter 15: Delivering the WOW!

After taking care of the patient's problem, the patient thanked Dr. Mary for her service and asked for her business card. Dr. Mary handed the patient one of her business cards and thanked the patient for his kind words. The patient replied, "You don't understand. I would like many of your cards. You have provided me with outstanding service and it is my desire to repay the effort. I own seven salons and it is my intention to provide your card to all of my customers."

Dr. Mary didn't just create a new patient, she created an ambassador. Ambassadors are those individuals who gladly spread the word about your services. Ambassadors are worth their weight in gold, as they make it their point to tell everyone about their experiences, both good and bad. What's interesting is that everyone can be an ambassador — if they're wowed!

In his great marketing book, *The Tipping Point: How Little Things Can Make a Big Difference,* Malcolm Gladwell describes how just a few key individuals are at the heart of the success of any business. These individuals spread the word about a business in such a way that, at a specific, definable moment, the business experiences a tipping point and explodes.[1]

Patients may come to you for an eye health exam or eyewear. But they will return to you year in and year out — and they'll refer others — only if they're WOWed. Think of yourself as a consumer. What causes you to shout from the rooftops about a product or service? It isn't about satisfaction; it's about a memorable experience.

---

1 Malcolm Gladwell, *The Tipping Point: How Little Things Can Make a Big Difference* (Boston: Little, Brown and Company, 2000).

Satisfying patients isn't enough in today's world. What creates sustainability and referrals is doing something remarkable — something memorable. Seth Godin, in his wonderful book *Purple Cow: Transform Your Business by Being Remarkable,* dubbed these remarkable actions "Purple Cows."[2] Seth teaches us all about transforming our businesses by doing something remarkable.

Creating a WOW isn't rocket science. Just look around you. What excites you as a consumer? What causes you to talk about another's product or service? Was it the free sample of chocolate handed to you at Godiva? Or the waitress who remembered how you take your coffee? Most of the time, if you think about it carefully, WOWs are created or destroyed by small acts. Consider these two situations:

First is a story that was originally posted on my blog within two hours of the experience:

Customer Service Hazards in a Wired World

This is a story about customer service, the danger of "no," and the amazing power of the Internet.

About an hour ago (remember that — just an hour ago) I left a conference in New York City. The event was offered by *Consulting* Magazine, which is owned by Kennedy Information out of Peterborough, NH. Entitled "Consulting Summit 2008," this was a gathering of about 150 owners of consulting firms

---

2 Seth Godin, *Purple Cow: Transform Your Business by Being Remarkable* (New York: Portfolio, 2003).

and was mostly comprised of larger consultancies. Names like IBM, Proudfoot, and American Express seemed to dominate the attendee list.

I invested $895 for this one-day wonder, which I must admit I found interesting and valuable. Indeed, I was one of 20 people who sprung an additional $495 for a lunch that included a very mediocre buffet and a review of the findings from Kennedy's research "The Best Firms to Work For" delivered by the Editor in Chief of *Consulting* Magazine. I was one of 20 people in the room with the presenter, so I guess that makes me a "Top 20 Customer" of the conference. File this fact away.

The speakers and content were good. Like many of these events, the sponsoring organization used the event to position some of its services. Kennedy publishes a lot of research on the consulting industry and, indeed, has a consultancy themselves. Their clients are firms like mine — and some much larger — that seek to improve their business. Even consultants hire consultants. I was interested in their services and so voiced my interest to their strategic accounts manager. I was informed that the firm could handle my needs and was introduced to one of their consultants. We agreed to follow up after the conference to explore a relationship. File this fact away as well.

It was clearly evident that there were only a few small consulting firms represented at the conference. Further, I was alone in New York City for the evening and desired to meet up with some of the attendees to talk shop. So, being the ever-resourceful individual that I am, at the afternoon break, I asked the moderator (the same editor-in-chief who presented my noon experience) if he could make a short announcement for me at the end of the day. I even gave him a written script and it was implied that my request was not a problem. The script read as follows:

"Al Cleinman owns a small, specialized consulting group and is interested in connecting with a few CEOs of smaller firms for dinner following this event to share ideas. If you're interested, please meet him during the cocktail hour following this session."

Well, the meeting ended and the moderator failed to make my announcement. I immediately approached him and asked him why. His response: "It was nixed." I probed further, asking him, "Why would my simple request be denied?" He informed me, very directly — almost caustically — that he didn't have to tell me and it was basically none of my business.

Now, what made this response so amazing was that the last session of the day was focused on delivering on customer desires. Go figure!

Mine was a request for a 15-second announcement to accommodate a simple desire. It was obviously important to me, as I provided two hours' notice and a script. I would have gladly done it myself if it was a hassle. Was this not a harmless request? Was this not a no-cost request? The way the moderator informed me of the decision was as if it were something of strategic significance. I imagined the entire board of directors huddled in a corner discussing the pros and cons of my request, using decision support software to arrive at "No!"

Whoever made the decision to nix my very simple request could have so easily accommodated me and dramatically enhanced my value quotient and, perhaps, that of others. Further, my request would certainly not have negatively impacted the program; it was over! Instead, I walked away from investing $1,300 feeling less than enthused — indeed, angry. It took just 15 seconds of a nine-hour day to destroy my otherwise positive experience.

So amazed was I about this that I approached the consultant from Kennedy who was pitching my business. I returned his card with an explanation that I had no interest in doing business with a firm that thought so little of a simple customer service request; that I choose not to do business with a firm that says "no" when "yes" would have been so easy. Even worse, I told him, was that they failed to provide any explanation for the seemingly ludicrous decision (after all, if it was some major issue, I'm a reasonable guy and would have understood). For want of a very small act, *poof* went a potential multi-thousand dollar client.

And this was billed as the "Networking Event of the Year."

So, what's my message?

1. Never say "no" to a reasonable request; when in doubt, do what's right by the customer. Always.

2. Empower your team to say "yes" and stand by them.

3. Identify what's important to your customer — it may not be what you think — and give it to them.

4. As with the great restaurant experience that's destroyed because the check took too long to arrive, watch the little stuff — it's often more important than the big stuff.

5. In our wired world, bad news travels very, very fast to many, many people (this blog entry will likely be viewed by over 5,000 people)! Make sure that your news is positive.

Contrast the above experience with the following experience I also posted on my blog within days of its occurrence:

Dillards Department Store and the Cleinman "WOW" Award

This past Monday, while visiting my brother, I purchased a new suitcase at the Dillards in Mesa, Arizona. While I call upstate NY home, it's not unusual for me to do my shopping on the road — after all, it's where I spend the majority of my time and the pickins are slim where I live. As you can imagine, with my travel schedule, I need a good suitcase. My last one hit the million mile mark and started to disintegrate.

I packed up my new bag and headed for home. Upon arrival, I noticed that the outside zipper was broken. Given my need for quality, I didn't have confidence that this bag was going to work for me and I simply don't have time for trial and error. I wanted to return the suitcase for credit, but I was a long way from a Dillards.

So, putting on my "customer from hell" hat and preparing for a fight, I called the Dillards in Mesa and spoke to Neil, the manager of the luggage department. My conversation took no more than three minutes.

AHC: "I purchased a piece of luggage from you on Monday and used it once. The zipper has broken."

Neil: "Well, just return it and we'll give you a new one."

AHC: "That's a problem on two fronts. First, I won't be in Phoenix anytime soon and second, I don't really trust the piece, given that it broke on its first run."

Neil: "OK, go to your receipt and read me the 10-digit number at the top. I'll just credit your account."

AHC: "That's great! How do I get the bag back to you?"

Neil: "Just throw it away, keep it, or give it away. No sense spending money on shipping."

WOW!

Neil, to put it mildly, I'm still blown away by our conversation and your no-nonsense, customer-centric approach. I was prepared for a hassle — or at least the need to pack the bag up and ship it to Arizona. You didn't just try to satisfy me; no, you WOWed me! You took the wind right out of my sails.

Congratulations! Today I award you an Al Cleinman "WOW Award." As a professional speaker, I spend a good deal of my year talking about the topic of customer service to audiences throughout North America. I am now a Dillards ambassador. You and your team — both up and down the corporate ladder — can rest assured that your gesture to me will be repaid. This WOW experience will be shared from the podium with thousands of individuals for many, many years to come.

Congratulations, Neil and Dillards. You've got an ambassador in Al Cleinman and a customer for life.

The preceding two stories clearly demonstrate both sides of the WOW experience. What might you do in your business to take what would be perceived as a customer hassle and turn it into a service goldmine? Are your employees empowered to do what's necessary to create a WOW? Why not?

CHAPTER 16

Know Your Numbers

I remember the words as if they were said to me just yesterday instead of way back in 1984. Millard Roberts was then working for me as an analyst, largely on a volunteer basis (he wouldn't accept money). Bob, as he liked to be called, was not your typical hourly employee. At the time, Bob was 65 and quite the eccentric individual with a unique and controversial history. He had graduated from Yale with a degree in divinity and had been a well-regarded minister in New York City in the 1960s. He had been appointed president of Parson's College in Fairfield, Iowa, and, during his 12-year tenure, took enrollment from about 250 students to more than 6,000. He also presided over Parson's precipitous decline. Along the way, he created a unique educational experiment that broke controversial ground on a number of innovations still in existence today. He'd even been featured in *Life* magazine.

One day, Bob was studying the production in our surfacing lab and, after some review, discovered an improvement opportunity. I was amazed at his meticulously detailed green spreadsheets of numbers and notes; at the time, I had little understanding of what the numbers meant. That afternoon, Bob said to me — in his characteristic gravelly voice —words that I will never forget: "If you look at numbers long enough, they'll start talking to you."

In many respects, Bob's message to me became the foundation of all that we do at Cleinman Performance Partners. It was through Bob's teachings that I learned the concept of benchmarking. It was through his mentoring that I was first exposed to open-book management and the power of sharing information with one's team.

Tracking performance and understanding how the various areas of your business contribute to your income is a fundamental business tool without which any business will wallow in inefficiency and court demise. Numbers provide the facts without which one must rely on conjecture.

It is unfortunate that there exists so much confusion about numbers in the accounting world. This confusion is the result of a fundamental conflict over objectives. One's business objective is to maximize profits. But your accountant's objective is to minimize your taxes. As a result, professionals are encouraged to report their income using cash-basis accounting as opposed to accrual-basis accounting. The resultant accounting system, while simple and tax beneficial, can actually hide fundamental economic problems within your practice.

The difference between cash- and accrual-basis accounting has to do with the time frame in which revenues and expenses are recorded and reported. And, while your accountant will likely tell you that cash-basis accounting will suffice, I believe that accountants who provide such counsel are dead wrong. Accrual-basis accounting will give a far more accurate picture of the results of your business operations.

Yes, cash-basis accounting is a very simple form of accounting. When a payment is received from patients or payors, the revenue is recorded as of the date of the receipt of funds no matter when the sale was made. Checks are written when funds are available to pay bills, and the expense is recorded as of the check date regardless of when the expense was incurred.

With cash-basis accounting, revenue is recorded when received and expenses are recorded when paid.

Accrual-basis accounting matches revenues to the time period in which they are earned and expenses to the time period in which they are incurred. While a bit more complex than cash-basis accounting, this method provides critical information about your business that is otherwise masked. For instance, cash-basis accounting would have you recording your vision plan payments as your income and would disregard the massive write-offs. This then masks results such as declines in your gross profit margins.

The accrual method allows you to match revenues to the expenses incurred in earning them, giving you more meaningful financial reports.

In today's vision plan and managed care environment — with as much as 50 percent of gross charges being written off

— having accurate financial information is critical to success. Further, your business will be more successful when each member of your team understands how their individual activities impact the financial success of the enterprise.

One doesn't have to wait until the end of a period and the generation of an income statement or balance sheet to understand what's going on in your business. Indeed, daily measurement of activity may be the only way one can consistently drive the practice forward. For instance, each day and with each patient, certain things must occur for you to be profitable. If you are open 20 days per month and your overhead is $20,000, then you must generate $1,000 in gross profit daily in order to break even. If your average patient generates $200 in gross profit, then you must see five patients each day to break even. Each and every day! Each and every patient! Thus, the management of your practice can be broken down into what I term "actionable numbers." Each member of your team should have specific, actionable numbers assigned to them and tracked by them. For example, if you have 16 comprehensive appointment slots available on a given day, then your front desk coordinator should be focused on filling those slots. Their success can — and should — be scored daily. The same applies to your opticians. They can be scored on capture rate (pairs of lenses sold per comprehensive exam) and average sale (gross optical charges per comprehensive exam).

Your team will rally around their own performance when objective measurements are used. When you track good data and make that data available to your team, your practice will perform better.

CHAPTER 17

Working Smarter, Not Harder

"I need to hire an associate. I'm working five days a week and grossing $700,000. I don't have a life and I need help managing my business."

In a variety of ways, I've heard these words hundreds of times. You're working hard. Perhaps you're even making good money. But it's likely you're not earning what you think you should, and you're burned out.

Many people confuse activity with success. Further, many of you look at time in absolute terms, not in terms of productivity.

Dr. Frank sees patients four days a week and every other Saturday. He's a busy guy with a $600,000 practice. He sees between six and eight full exams a day but has the capacity for 14. In between patients, he handles administrative tasks, marketing, bookkeeping, etc. On the surface, Dr. Frank operates just like his colleagues. He sees patients and manages his business. A deeper review confirms what the numbers indicate; Dr. Frank actually has many holes in his schedule. Several times a day, he picks up 20 minutes here and 15 minutes there.

Dr. Frank sees this as valuable administrative time. We characterize this time as "garbage time." The reality is that it's impossible to develop a highly productive practice in between patients. Leadership and practice development take time, and Dr. Frank's schedule only provides relatively unproductive moments that actually increase his stress. There's a better way.

Our first objective is to balance capacity with demand. We accomplish this by crunching Dr. Frank's patient schedule down to three patient care days a week. He now schedules patients Monday, Tuesday, and Wednesday of week one and Thursday, Friday, and Saturday of week two. This allows him to provide patients with appointments on any day they desire. On days that he's not scheduled to see patients, his staff manages all the administrative tasks, special testing, and eyewear delivery (which is now handled by appointment).

In addition, Dr. Frank now has a full day each week for administrative work and staff meetings. There's a significant bonus with his change — he gets to enjoy a five-day weekend every two weeks. The result is that Dr. Frank has an easier life. He and his team are less stressed. Patients actually receive a higher level of service, and Dr. Frank has the time necessary to create and plan the programs which will deliver his desired growth. One year later, his revenue is up by 15 percent.

Many optometrists confuse technical work with leadership. Yes, as a professional, you sell your time and your desire is to have a full schedule. But by eliminating the holes in your schedule and actually blocking time to work on the business, you become more productive. You and your team can focus on developing the business when you have the time to do so. Otherwise, developing your business becomes something you do in between patients, and that's just not productive.

Abraham Lincoln once said, "Give me six hours to chop down a tree and I will spend the first four sharpening the axe."[1] Likewise, if I have a one-hour job to do, I'll spend 45 minutes planning it.

Time management is a critical element of your business and your life. Some of us are good at it while others have a significant weakness in this area. For me, time management starts first with understanding myself, my natural behaviors, and what I describe as my peaks and valleys. Specific types of work seem to be easier for me at certain times of day. For instance, I know that I'm most creative in the morning. Therefore, I provide myself with time in the morning to think. This is also my best writing time. I also know that I'm best at detailed work — such as crunching numbers or writing analytical documents — in the early afternoon or late at night.

After many years of self-observation, I also know that I don't do well with interruptions. My attention to detail is not a natural strength. Thus, when I'm working on a project, I know that it takes a concerted effort for me to concentrate. That's why, many years ago, I stopped taking unscheduled phone calls and allowing interruptions to my work.

---

1 "QuotationReference.com." QuotationReference.com. http://www.quotationreference.com/quotefinder.php?strt=1&subj=Abraham Lincoln&byax=1.

Most every meeting and phone call that I have is scheduled in advance by my assistant. This allows me to avoid interruptions, which are highly stressful to me. A further benefit of this methodology is that our firm has moved from one that was highly reactive (I need to solve this problem now) to highly proactive (what can we do to change the system to avoid a problem). Simply put, I don't allow interruptions to my work day, and that forces me and my team to be more proactive.

Many optometrists are people pleasers. You've been successful because you strive to help every patient anytime, anywhere — as you should. This behavior often extends to community involvement. I have many clients that are on multiple boards of directors and otherwise deeply involved in their community. When asked, their tendency is to say "yes" for fear that saying "no" will hurt their business. These are often the same individuals who report a high level of stress.

While volunteering for your community and your profession is an important obligation, it's as important to say "no" as it is to say "yes." Learn when enough is enough. Learn that you can be involved in many ways with organizations beyond volunteering your time. When you spread yourself too thin, your ability to contribute is limited. Busy doesn't translate to effective.

Identify how to improve your own productivity by stepping back and really attempting to understand yourself, how you think, and how you work. Learning how to say no while offering other members of your team the opportunity to support a cause will both expand your reach and also build the skills of your team members.

"Sarah, I'd love to participate on your board, but I'm simply overbooked. If you're open to it, I'd like to see if one of our team members would be interested. I'd be happy to support their involvement with some time and a contribution to your cause. In fact, our senior optician, Dan, has an interest in your cause and would make a fine contributor to your board."

CHAPTER 18

Are You Partner Material?

You're driving on the expressway, tooling along with your cruise control set at 74 mph (the maximum "safe from a ticket" speed). You come upon a driver in the left lane. He's going 60 mph — well below the speed limit — riding along comfortably next to another car that's traveling at the same speed. Neither car is pulling ahead; they're just tracking each other. As you pull up on his tail, you shout to no one in particular, "Don't you know that the left-hand lane is for passing?!" You flash your lights, hoping the dude will step on the gas and pull ahead of the car to the right and let you by.

But they don't react to your not-so-subtle message. For miles, you're stuck behind traffic that doesn't want to pass or go as fast as you'd like. It doesn't take long for you to be seething inside. You shout expletives. You flash your lights repeatedly. You pull behind the car in the right-hand lane, hoping they'll both get the message. Try as you might, neither of the cars in front of you will take the action necessary for you to pass. And, indeed, you can actually see the driver in the left lane smiling at you in his rear view mirror, knowing full well that he's in control of you. How does this make you feel?

What I describe above is symbolic of a bad partnership. A partnership, like marriage, is a total commitment. Unfortunately, most partnerships — and I've seen many — are not built on a solid foundation.

What makes for a successful partnership? Why do some partnerships thrive while many end in turmoil and dissolution? For more than 30 years, I've observed and participated in partnerships in the vision care industry. I've personally known the power of a successful partnership and the heartbreak of one gone awry. In my consulting practice, I've assisted hundreds of optometrists in piecing partnerships together, and I've structured and negotiated numerous separations.

One thing is for certain: If you've seen one partnership, you've seen just one. No two relationships are alike. The dynamics of diversity are the glue that holds successful partnerships together. However, among all the contrasts are 10 common denominators exhibited by successful partnerships.

Successful Partners Have a Shared Vision

Before you jump on the highway to partnership, make sure that all parties have a similar destination in mind. What are your individual visions about the future? A good exercise is to independently write down your visions for the practice five and 10 years out. Then compare: Are your visions similar or diametrically opposed? Analyze your prospective partner's attitudes about people and change. Do they exhibit personality traits that you admire? Is your prospective partner a team player or dictatorial? What is their attitude towards change and personal development? What about your prospective partner's energy level? Will tasks be reasonably shared, or is your prospective partner a nine-to-fiver? While individual personality traits can be very different, partners must have common goals and share equitably the work necessary to achieve them.

Friends Don't Necessarily Make Good Partners

Dr. George and Dr. Steve were best friends in college. Dr. George dreamed of opening a practice and having Dr. Steve join him. They talked endlessly of the fun they could have by practicing together. After school, they each went their separate ways. Dr. George purchased a small practice and proceeded to build a thriving business. Dr. Steve went to work for a retail chain. They kept in touch, sharing an occasional vacation together and continuing their dialogue about practicing together. Several years later, Dr. George, who by then had a thriving practice, sought out Dr. Steve and convinced him to join as a partner.

To entice Dr. Steve to join him, Dr. George promised a salary higher than what Dr. Steve was currently earning. And of course, there would be a car and other perks associated with private practice. The partnership that developed was based on a personal relationship. Compensation was based on personal desire as opposed to productivity. But the practice didn't grow enough to support the additional partner. The reality was that Dr. George and Dr. Steve had very different energy levels. Dr. George was driven to be successful while Dr. Steve placed more importance on his outside hobbies. Even though they were best friends, Dr. George became very critical of Dr. Steve (but not to his face).

Because of the friendship and the structure of the relationship, Dr. George didn't feel comfortable addressing the problems in their formative stages. And Dr. Steve began to resent Dr. George's success. "Partners share everything," he thought. But neither party would openly discuss their true thoughts for fear they'd hurt their personal relationship. The partnership never quite made it and, ultimately, disbanded. Both the partnership and the relationship were destroyed in the process. Good partnerships are built first on a solid business footing with a clear shared vision. Prior close friendship often inhibits the open and direct communication necessary to build a true partnership.

Good Partnerships Have Balance

We can't all be good at everything. The most successful partnerships are ones in which each participant represents a unique set of qualities and qualifications. One partner may have strong analytical skills while the other is marketing oriented. One may love contact lens practice, the other may be intrigued by dry eye. One may have an effusive personality, the other is reserved. Good partners act as alter egos. Opposites do attract, and opposites can make for successful partners. Laurel and Hardy, Jobs and Wosniak, Rodgers and Hammerstein: All are examples of successful partnerships comprised of very different individuals. But partners, no matter how diverse in personality and technical interest, must share a common vision and a common set of values. Balanced personalities and technical skills combined with a shared vision are the building blocks of a successful relationship.

Successful Partners Share a Relationship Beyond the Office

Partners who don't enjoy a periodic dinner, show, or ballgame together may not understand each other as people. A solid non-office relationship builds mutual understanding and trust. This empathy is necessary in order to work out the inevitable differences that crop up from time to time. Without a relationship beyond the office — without a family-to-family connection — partners won't have an understanding of the viewpoints of a partner's family. Pressures brought by influences outside the partnership are often at the heart of discord. A partnership should build a degree of friendship, but friends rarely make good partners.

Communication is Everything

If there's something on your mind, say it! When your partner says something, listen! All successful relationships are based on good communications, and successful communicators know how to speak up — and how to listen. Most partnerships that end in dissolution, like most marriages that end in divorce, arrive there because the partners stopped working on the relationship. Discord and disagreement are inevitable, and the only way to move beyond the issues is to seek resolution through open communication. Meet with your partners regularly. Look for every opportunity to discuss issues. Talk often, even if it's about the weather. I know one multi-location partnership that installed two-way radios in their partners' cars (long before cellphones) so they could jointly review the day's activities on their way home each night. The radios allowed for constant communications in between periodic partner meetings. Talk may be cheap, but it's the currency of a good relationship.

Behind Every Good Partnership is a Well-Written Agreement

While no one bases a relationship on a written document, well-constructed agreements document each party's understanding of the relationship as well as define the relationship in legal terms. In effect, such agreements are guidelines for the life of the relationship. But it's not the agreements that are necessarily important, it's the process. Whether you're structured as a corporation or as a partnership, the elements of written agreements are really the same. You need a partnership or shareholders' agreement that spells out what will happen in the event a partner leaves (either by choice, by force, or by death or disability) and an operating agreement that defines how you will manage the business.

Such an agreement should also define governance. How will the partnership/corporation operate? Who has final authority and over what matters? A partnership/shareholder agreement and operating agreement should spell out all the details of the relationship and what happens if the relationship is to be dissolved. In addition to the partnership/shareholder agreement, each professional member of the team should have an employment agreement. This spells out compensation matters and work-related responsibilities and defines the individual partner's work relationship with the partnership. As you work through the often complicated process of defining the terms of these agreements, seek win-win arrangements. And when the agreements are completed, file them away. Hopefully, you'll never need them.

Ownership and Compensation are Not Related

Just because you're a 50 percent owner (or 30 percent or 90 percent) doesn't mean that you should take income in proportion to your ownership stake. Generally, personal production must be measured and must be the basis for the majority of compensation. Also, successful partners recognize that each individual brings a unique set of skills to the relationship. These professional and managerial skills must be valued for compensation purposes. Compensation plans should be devised to be flexible and nonrestrictive. Keep base salaries as low as possible and representative of managerial responsibilities. The balance of cash flow after partner base salaries should be split based on production and ownership. Show me a partnership that pays for performance and I'll show you a partnership that performs.

Nepotism is for Soloists

I know of many instances in which family members are a practice's most skilled and motivated team players. However, when a partnership is involved, jealousy and criticism by non-family partners can eat away at even the strongest relationships. It's virtually impossible to treat a partner's family equally, so it's best to avoid the measurement problem. If you have a solo practice that employs a family member and you're about to take on a partner, take great care. Use the opportunity to review the performance of the family member and consider a change. Of course, you must fully disclose the relationship to prospective partners up front. In practices where a son or daughter is expected to become part of the professional team, encourage the family member to seek outside experience first. That way, everyone benefits from outside experience prior to partnership. Above all, treat family members equally and make sure compensation is commensurate with performance.

You Can't Share Responsibility and Authority

Football teams have only one quarterback; partnerships must have the same. Even equal partnerships must have one member who has ultimate decision-making authority. Just as in team sports, the smoothest working partnerships define areas of responsibility and authority for each player. The various areas of practice management (personnel, training, purchasing, marketing, finance, etc. are divided among the owners, and each calls the shots in those specific areas. Just as with staff, performance criteria should be established by the senior partner (or board of directors), and the managing partner's performance should be measured against these pre-established standards. Each department must have a champion. Management by committee usually doesn't work.

Trust is Essential

Most partnerships evolve. Often, a partnership is comprised of experienced senior partner(s) and junior partner(s). Partnerships that work involve a high degree of trust among the individual players. The senior partner must share responsibility and authority and allow the junior partner to develop skills. More often than not, managerial skills are developed through experience, and experience requires mistakes. Trust your partners to do the best job they can. Avoid criticism or unsolicited advice. Develop an environment of continual learning and change. Encourage your partners (and team) to take prudent risk. Celebrate mistakes as opportunities for learning. Above all, be flexible.

Partnerships are not always pretty. A successful partnership, like a successful marriage, is comprised of highs and lows, love and conflict, stress and relief. The relationship must be fluid; all parties must embrace change as a friend. Associations must be designed so all parties can win even if their individual contributions are very different.

Above all, agreements — whether partner or employee — should be worked out in advance. It's very difficult to develop a "prenup" after the "marriage."

CHAPTER 19

Better to Copy Genius than to Invent Mediocrity

The solution to virtually every problem has been identified somewhere by somebody. Every conceivable service has a specialist — an expert. Want a new logo? There are websites that will deliver dozens of proposals within days. Want a mortgage? You can have five proposals within the hour. Need to find the best source for new telephones? A quick search will provide you with everything you need to know. Looking for a restaurant? You'll find the best choice on your smartphone.

Just a decade ago, seeking out information, identifying resources, and finding solutions was both challenging and time-consuming. But in today's wired world, massive amounts of information are available through a simple Google search. Against this backdrop, it amazes me how many of us spend massive amounts of time and energy working on improvements that others have already achieved.

Many professionals never achieve their true capabilities because they and their teams adopt what is often referred to as a "not invented here" (NIH) attitude about their business. Further, as a society, we attach high value to individuals who create, while those who copy are often stigmatized. But, as the adage goes, "It is better to copy genius than to invent mediocrity."

Sam Walton, the great retailer, was quick to reveal where he got many of his best ideas — from his competitors. He'd say that he just took a good idea and made it better. That, in my opinion, is the essence of success — learning from others and applying continuous improvement to existing, proven strategies. And the best teachers are our customers and our peers.

Napoleon Hill, the father of the "personal success" genre of literature, studied the attributes of individuals such as Andrew Carnegie, John D. Rockefeller, and Henry Ford. In his bellwether book, *Think and Grow Rich,* Hill introduces his readers to the concept of the mastermind group.[1] In simple terms, a mastermind group is a group of like-minded individuals who meet on a regular basis to discuss ideas, explore opportunities, and solve each other's challenges. These groups are now mainstream and can be found in a number of forms and formats. My company operates Cleinman Performance Network, which is now comprised of over two dozen individual mastermind groups for both optometrist owners and selected staff positions (managers and opticians). Founded in 1999, the organization represents a highly systematized methodology for peers to learn from peers as well as thought leaders from both inside and outside our industry. The Network addresses industry issues head-on

---

1 Napoleon Hill, *Think and Grow Rich Original 1937 Edition* (S.l.: Duke Classics, 2012).

and well in advance of mainstream optometry, thus providing members with a unique perspective on their business as well as tools to stay ahead of the competition. Participants have access to specialists with expertise in virtually every area of business.

If you can think of it, the odds are that someone else has already perfected it.

So, the next time you're tempted to start from scratch on any project, consider first who else may have already devised a solution. As CEO of your enterprise, become disciplined in leveraging your organization's skills with both borrowed knowledge and outside experts and expertise.

CHAPTER 20

The Art of the Deal

During the course of your career, there will be occasions when you will negotiate some sort of deal. The situations are many:

- Employment
- Becoming a partner in a practice
- Purchasing a practice
- Merging with another practice
- Hiring an associate
- Selling a practice

In each of these situations and others not mentioned, there are myriad opportunities and pitfalls. Over many years in the dealmaking business, I have observed that optometrists are prone to making significant misjudgments in this area. These misjudgments are generally the result of a lack of experience. Dealmaking is an art form, and a significant portion of the dealmaking process is balancing opportunity manifestation with risk management.

Whether on the opportunity side or the risk side, the key to accomplishing your objectives is awareness. Awareness takes exposure. Just as your professional skills develop from observing thousands of situations, so, too, do dealmaking skills. However, the reality is that you can't afford to make mistakes in dealmaking; one wrong move and you can commit professional suicide. Thus, my first rule of dealmaking is:

Don't Go It Alone

Dealmaking is all about relationship design. While there are always technical components (how much, who does what, etc.), relationships are about energy. Relationships are not black and white, and they're not built strictly on numbers or assigned tasks. Relationships are built on trust; they ebb and flow based on the energy of the participants. And it takes experience to identify in advance how the energy of a relationship may evolve. In some respects, a good dealmaker has the perspective to figuratively read the tea leaves and turn over the tarot cards to envision the future of the relationship.

In my conversations with optometry students, one of my key messages is that, as hard as it is, they should build up their capital in anticipation of hiring an advisor to help them with their first employment transaction. After working on hundreds of contracting challenges with young professionals, I'm convinced that the ability to make this investment is critical to building the right foundation for your career. Of course, you should avail yourself of any services offered by your school. And, if nothing else, find yourself a mentor or two with experience in dealmaking. But don't think that a friend with a little bit of experience — or even a non-specialized attorney or accountant — has the requisite skills to work out a successful relationship.

Dr. Owen was an employed associate and the designated successor to a senior partner. One day, the senior partner dropped dead. Dr. Owen and the widow worked out the purchase of the practice with the assistance of attorneys on both sides. The transaction design involved a significant purchase price and an ongoing performance payment. Contracts were drawn up and executed. But in spite of the fact that the documents were written by attorneys, the design used, while perfectly legal in the general business world, was illegal in the professional world. The local attorneys used by both sides simply didn't have the experience to recognize this nuance. The result was expensive litigation.

My message is simple: whether an employee or an outside advisor, it is critical to surround yourself with the very best. You'll be rewarded for your investment with not only a well-designed deal, but also with greater knowledge of the process.

Before you embark on any kind of transaction, it's important to think strategically. There are a few questions that I use to help lead my thinking:

- What are you really trying to accomplish?

- What is the right way to accomplish it?

- Are you partnership material?

Sarah is a young OD with a busy practice. She's currently grossing $700,000 seeing patients four days a week. She's comfortable and in control — a Type A personality. She inquires about seeking a partner. "I'm busy and I need assistance with managing my practice," she says. "I just don't have the time to do all that needs to be done. I need a partner."

Sarah is strong-willed and loves to be in control. What Sarah needs is an experienced manager, not a partner.

Jordan is a 62-year-old OD with a small practice grossing only $400,000. He nets about $75,000 for his efforts. "I want to hire an associate so that I can retire when I'm 65," he says.

What Jordan needs is to build his practice profitability now, maximize his performance, and then do an outright sale. Hiring an OD will only drain his income and resources in the short term, resulting in a lower value for the practice.

Joseph and Martha are 30-something ODs who own a single-location practice grossing over $2 million per year. The practice is located in a beautiful facility which they own. They're good leaders and partners and have an outstanding staff. They've enjoyed a history of year-over-year growth. "We need to bring on another partner, as we're growing and have the need for more capacity," they explained.

Joseph and Martha have done all the heavy lifting to build their practice. They've made considerable time and monetary investments to get their ship where it is. There's no need to share the results of their hard-fought gains with a partner. Further, a third party entering a family partnership is cause for trouble. What they need — at least for now — is an employed associate, not a partner.

Choosing the right strategy for your specific situation is critical to your success. Often — just as you experience with some patients — what you think you need is not what you really need.

Whether you're buying or selling, hiring or being hired, you're engaged in a dealmaking process. Here are some hard-earned tips:

- **Do your homework.** What is it that you want to accomplish? Is this the right way? What are the alternatives? What are your concerns? What are the nonnegotiables?

- **Listen.** What does the other party want to accomplish? What are they trying to get out of the deal? What are their concerns? What are their nonnegotiables?

- **Design.** What are the elements of the deal? Who's going to do what? What is being purchased and for how much? What are the economics? What are the legal considerations (noncompetes, right of future purchase, etc.). What is the due diligence process?

- **Put it in writing.** Document the proposed transaction in the form of a term sheet or letter of intent — a short, generally nonbinding document that provides all the key elements of the transaction.

- **Negotiate.** There are two levels of negotiations. The first is on the deal itself, which is generally driven by the term sheet. With this document, you have a valuable tool to guide the back and forth of negotiations. When you agree on something, get it off the table. Focus on what you disagree on. Ratchet down the deal. The second level of negotiations will come when the legal documents are prepared, and these negotiations should be limited to contracting language (does the contract reflect the intent of the deal as outlined in the memorandum of terms).

- **Perform due diligence.** Once you have the term sheet completed and executed, it's time to confirm that the information you've been provided is accurate. In a capital transaction such as a purchase, this step includes reviewing the assets and financials, interviewing employees, reviewing patient records, etc. What you're seeking in the due diligence process is confirmation that you're making the right decision based on accurate information.

- **Close the deal.** Once due diligence is complete, documents are finalized, and financing is in place, it's time to ink the deal and sign all the papers. There may be some last-minute negotiations as specific outlying issues come to the table. Never give in to a demand placed on the table at the last minute. Walk away, even for a few hours, so you can think through the ramifications of the request and ascertain if the demand is an early warning indicator of how the other party operates.

Remorse and Reality

Now the deal is done and the champagne has been poured. You'll likely have second thoughts and also uncover things that weren't anticipated. The reality is that your contracts are in place to protect you on the downside. On virtually a daily basis, you'll uncover operational realities that you'll have to deal with outside the agreement. If you do come across something that needs to be changed, move to change it. Don't wait or simply ignore the issue. Also, one of your objectives is to have this remorse and reality period early in the deal. Spend time thinking about worst-case scenarios while in the design stage. This will help you cover things that you may not have otherwise documented.

Valuation

Another element of many deals is valuation. How much is the practice worth? If you're the buyer, you'll want to pay as little as possible. If you're the seller, you'll want the opposite. Your natural inclination, as almost a first step, is to seek an independent fair market valuation of the assets in question. While there are a number of elements to the valuation process, the reality is that, in most deals, value comes about as a result of the deal-making process. It's not really a starting point but an end point. Valuation is not a science but an art form. While some accountants do valuation work, they are generally not dealmakers and typically take a mathematical approach to valuations. But the reality is that, in any purchase, you're really only buying three things:

- **A cash-generating machine.** Focus your valuation process on cash flow and operating income. In general, the more cash the business generates, the more you can afford to pay for it. Hard assets are secondary to cash flow.

- **An opportunity for growth.** If the practice hasn't demonstrated historical growth, why would it grow after you make the purchase? What are the underlying operating ratios that would indicate opportunity? What assets are being underutilized? What markets are being underserved?

- **A lifestyle.** Many professionals make the mistake of focusing on the specific opportunity instead of on the lifestyle the opportunity represents. If you can't see yourself living and thriving in a particular community, don't do the deal. Don't look at the purchase as just an asset — you're going to spend a significant amount of time and energy building it, so you'd better enjoy the community where you reside.

Any deal is the result of a negotiation process. Here are some negotiating considerations:

- **What do I give, what do I get?** Be prepared to answer these questions for all parties in the transaction, including secondary-level parties. For instance, you may clearly understand what you get out of a transaction and what your future partner will get. But how will the deal impact the office manager? What about your respective spouses or vendors, etc.?

- **Put time on your side.** Never allow yourself to be placed in the position of having to do anything. When time is on your side in a negotiation, you have a much better chance of coming out on top. But, more importantly, the odds that you'll make an error are significantly reduced. Deals take time. Even simple deals have as many as six parties involved (you, the other side, and both of your accountants and attorneys). Even a simple employment contract can take six months to develop and execute. Don't be caught short on time.

- **Document the deal.** Every transaction, partner relationship, and employment relationship should be backed by a written agreement (yes, even at-will employees should have a work agreement). If you can't get an agreement completed, odds are that you're going to have a problem downstream. I've heard this response on many occasions: "Yes, we have a contract; it's just never been signed." Well, an unsigned contract is just a collection of thoughts. Get it signed!

- **Too many cooks spoil the broth.** While earlier in this chapter I recommend surrounding yourself with good advisors, the inverse can be a problem, too. Dealmaking is an art form. As with all art forms, the process is subjective. There are no rules except on the tax and legal side — and even those are often subject to interpretation. Thus, if you find yourself having to negotiate conflicting opinions and you're not confident in your business skills, retain the services of one qualified individual to help you navigate these uncharted waters.

- **Always look for the win-win.** If you think you can pull the wool over the other party's eyes and get away with something, forget it. Likewise, if you are feeling that you're not getting the best situation for you, walk away. How individuals act in negotiations is very telling about the future of your relationship. In many respects, an employment agreement or transaction document is like a prenuptial agreement. If you can't work it out, odds are the relationship won't work either. Further, in today's litigant-hungry world, any deal is subject to turning ugly. If all parties to the transaction aren't focused on a balanced set of terms, then it's a good sign that the relationship will not evolve as you desire. Buyer beware!

At the end of the day, every transaction, every partnership, and every employment relationship is unique. Make sure you've done your homework. Never ever adopt someone else's contract or deal design as your own. Those types of actions are best left to consultants, attorneys and accountants.

CHAPTER 21

The Speed of the Leader

A common trap for optometrists is the perception that "I am my practice" — most business owners and professionals succumb to it at least once. After all, your name is on the door, you sign the checks, and, without you, there would be no practice. However, your practice could not survive in the absence of many other factors as well — most notably, your team. Your team represents your most important asset. And the difference between success and mediocrity is usually leadership.

Leadership can be defined by what happens when you're away. The manner in which you regard your practice, your patients, and your staff will determine your success. If you behave selfishly, your team will be inclined to do the same. You are the example. Below, you'll find some instances of how autocratic behavior can manifest itself. You may be surprised at how some of your actions can be interpreted and to what they may lead.

Taking cash. Some practitioners take cash from their practice as opposed to declaring it as income. This stems from the attitude of "It's my money, I earned it, and I'm not sharing it!" Remember, when someone spends 40 hours a week in your practice, there are no secrets. A sloppy bookkeeping system that allows you to take a little cash probably won't catch anyone else taking a little cash, either.

Your actions send the message: "Feel free to cheat." The result is that staff members won't feel guilty about helping themselves to the cash drawer since you do it, too. You also signal to the staff that it's okay to cut corners in other areas of the practice. The dangerous precedent you set (not to mention the legal risk you take!) is not worth the tax break.

Inconsiderate with time. Do you ever show up to the office five minutes late for an exam? Do you ever make patients wait while you're on the phone? Are you the first to go home at night? These actions tell your patients and staff, "My time is worth more than yours." Paying for your staff's time doesn't entitle you to waste it. It's difficult to credibly tell your team to place a high priority on patient service when you do not strive to serve patients promptly yourself. Your team will not be inclined to go the extra mile if you're out the door at five o'clock no matter what. Make patient care your first priority. If you are committed to your patients and your practice, your team will follow suit.

Abusiveness. One of the worst mistakes you can make is publicly reprimanding a staff member. Doing so embarrasses the staff member as well as other staff and patients who may be present. Again, this comes from an attitude towards the team of, "You're here to serve me. I pay you!" as opposed to "We're all here to serve the patient. They sign our checks!" A temperamental attitude demonstrates to your patients and staff a lack of caring and concern. You also show your staff that it is acceptable to lose control in the presence of patients. No one will trust the health of their eyes to someone who appears to be a bully. This type of behavior reduces confidence, which stifles the ability to delegate and further increases stress. Always handle your disagreements with staff calmly, reasonably, and in private.

Cheapness. Do you count every paper clip and postage stamp in your practice? Do you regard raises and bonuses for your team as a reward and incentive for good performance? Or rather as a "me versus them" battle for money? There is a vast difference between maintaining financial control and being a skinflint. People hate feeling nickel and dimed to death. Your staff will resent having to walk past your new Cadillac if they have to pay for their own coffee. Always look at the overall cost compared to the overall benefit, as the cost of a few extras is usually much lower than the cost of losing a patient or staff member. For example, staff training can be expensive; however, high turnover, low morale, and poor quality staff support is even more expensive. Empower your staff to take every reasonable measure to satisfy your patients. Find ways to reward your staff for good performance; the investment will pay off handsomely.

Another place to not be cheap is with adequate equipment. Frequently, doctors fail to provide the tools necessary for their staff to do a good job. Purchase of items such as computers, office furnishings, lab tools, and the like are frequently avoided since these items do not directly produce revenue. However, these tools improve efficiency, freeing staff time for more productive work. Look at the tools you currently provide for your team. Would you be able to perform superior work using them?

Clutter and Disorganization. Does your private office look like a disaster area? Many doctors treat their offices as their corner away from home to collect clutter and junk. Patient files, mail, journals and so forth are piled from floor to ceiling. I know of one doctor who unearthed 15-year-old journals and files for patients who had been deceased for over five years! It is impossible to expect your staff to keep the optical boutique spotless and the lab organized if you don't demonstrate the same level of concern in your area. Worse, valuable time is frequently consumed by doing battle with the paper monster on your desk. Treat every inch of your practice as though you had glass walls. The staff restroom should be as tidy and sanitary as the patient rest room. The staff lounge should not be the repository for practice junk. And your sidewalk and entrance should be cleared of debris each day. Professionalism is not a show you put on; it should be your attitude towards every element of your practice.

Leadership has more to do with who you are than with what you do. Take stock of your attitudes and behaviors and examine the messages they send. If these are attributes you would not want in your team, you should reconsider them yourself. Showing your team how to work — by your own example — is far more powerful than telling them. Imagine yourself as a member of your staff: What do you need to do the best possible job? How do you want to be treated and respected? What kind of environment do you want to work in? What would you expect from your leader?

Management can be delegated; leadership cannot. Your team will follow the tone you set for the practice no matter what you may dictate to the contrary. This does not mean you're not free to be human and make mistakes. It means that your actions need to reflect the attitudes you want shared by the whole practice. Remembering this important principle is an essential element of managing your success.

CHAPTER 22

Creating Wealth

From time to time, I've found myself at colleges of optometry providing insights to students into their chosen profession from a businessman's perspective. My workshop entitled "The Entrepreneurial Optometrist: Controlling your Destiny" is designed to help the next generation of optometrists manage their careers and their lives. Invariably, I'm asked the question, "What single piece of advice can you give us?" My standard response is, "Continue to live like students."

I came to this answer based on an actual experience. Early in my consulting career, I was contacted by a 42-year-young optometrist — we'll call him Dr. Bob — who asked me to sell his practice. I was quite surprised that such a young man would want to retire from the profession. "Why," I asked, "do you want to leave your profession?" "Because I can," was his answer. Bob and his wife had made a very good living over the prior decade. And, as he told me, they had "continued to live like students." Indeed, his income was fully five times that which he needed to live. During that decade — a single 10-year period — he and his wife had invested wisely. They had developed a portfolio that, even in a bad year, would produce dividends large enough to cover their living expenses. They had made bank and were now going to do what they wanted to do when they wanted to do it. They lived below their means and put their money to work for them.

In a similar vein, my dear friends Alan and Carol retired in their mid-40s. He had been an executive with an airline and she a flight attendant. Early in their careers, they had focused their attention on eliminating all debt and developing investable income. They had a very specific goal they wanted to reach — having a portfolio that would take care of their day-to-day income requirements. Both Alan and Carol became very skilled at stock trading. They drove used cars (and still do) and bought and fixed up properties for resale. They worked jobs they wanted to work, including for Disney and SeaWorld. When they wanted to see the South, they secured jobs as relief managers for a hotel chain, placing them in different communities for two weeks at a time. When they wanted to visit Hawaii, they bought a home there and, in a three-year period, more than doubled their investment. They lived large, if having fun and enjoying life are the measure. They're not out to impress anyone with trappings, yet they live very comfortably and have historically done what they want when they wanted. Most who know Alan and Carol are envious.

Contrast these two stories with the more common experience: as general business consultants, my firm invests time with clients to understand their goals, their personal balance sheets, and their retirement plans. More often than not, our clients have great income but little real wealth. This is typical among doctors of all kinds. They have cars and houses. They take amazing vacations. They eat out frequently. Their children go to the very best schools. But introduce a bad month or two — or a medical crisis — and they'd be bankrupt. They often invest what little excess cash they have in white elephant houses and investments in which they have little expertise. They have income, yet little wealth.

How does this happen? Our experience is that it starts out with the fact that doctors generally have ready access to credit, resulting in their living above their means. They buy a house they can ill afford. Then, along with the McMansion comes the need to purchase expensive furniture, often on credit. And, of course, they have to live up to their title; doctors have a certain standard of living. In addition, in today's world, many optometrists start out with hundreds of thousands of dollars in education debt. As a result, their income never catches up to their debt levels and they wake up in their late 50s or early 60s experiencing a "holy crap moment" wondering how they're going to replace their handsome income (and corresponding spending habits) in retirement. Today, many doctors are postponing retirement — largely because they don't have the funds necessary to live the lifestyle they desire without working. In a career during which the average optometrist will earn over five times that of an average worker, this seems a shame.

So, what to do? While everyone's situation is different, here are a few tips taken from a lifetime of observation:

- **Keep excellent records.** Get a program like Quicken and use it personally. If you aren't comfortable with finances, get help — now!

- **Pay yourself first.** Pay yourself a reasonable salary, even if you think you can't afford it. Don't use your business as a bank.

- **Save.** Even if it's only $10 a week. Always live below your means.

- **Maximize your retirement savings.** Compounding is an amazing tool. $35,000 set aside by age 25 turns into $500,000 at age 65, but only $130,000 if saved by age 45.

- **Keep an impeccable credit score.** Stay away from credit card debt.

- **Invest first in your practice, then elsewhere.** Your practice likely earns over 25 percent of revenue while companies like Exxon are happy with seven percent. Where can you find a better investment than your own practice?

- **Hide your money from yourself.** Use payroll savings to automatically set aside funds.

- **Don't buy individual stocks or be a trader.** Invest in mutual funds and forget about them (but do review your portfolio with an expert annually).

- **Invest in rental property.** Either directly or indirectly. Your own building is a good place to start.

- **Don't be in a rush to pay off student or business debt.** Paying off debt requires income, which in turn is taxed. The resulting taxes may starve you of capital that can be better deployed elsewhere.

- **Diversify your investments, but never speculate or take a flyer.** Leave speculative investment (funding a friend's idea, etc.) to professional investors. First in is never first out.

- **Teach your kids how to work and how to save.**

- **Never do your own deals.** Never buy or sell a practice on your own. Experience is the best teacher and you don't have either the experience or the time to learn.

- **Don't be penny wise and pound foolish.** Sometimes it pays to simply say "yes" so you can move on to more important things.

- **Be decisive.** Time is money.

The greatest fortunes have been made over long periods of time. You won't likely become an overnight internet-style billionaire in optometry, so don't look for the get-rich-quick approach. Invest in your practice (the best facility, the very best staff) and stay true to your brand. Follow the fundamentals and you'll find yourself with all the money you need when you need it.

CHAPTER 23

It's All About Trust

When I was in my early 20s, a friend of mine helped me to think through my values and document a series of expressions about my core beliefs. This exercise, which I encourage my clients to replicate, ultimately evolved into a series of short sayings. One of these quotations has been especially important to me over the years:

> *People deserve your trust. What you sow, you reap tenfold.*

Having thought about values and looked back over my life, it's clear to me that this one word — trust — has the most significant impact on defining all for which we stand and on our life's ultimate outcome.

Like many, I have trusted others and been sorely burned. I have been the victim of embezzlement, outright theft, lying, and cheating. I've had my share of negative interactions and have had many reasons to become a cynic — to succumb to a closeted world that hides behind locked doors, guarded conversations, and attorneys. In business, how much of our energy do we consume verifying information or writing airtight contracts so as not to get burned? How often do we check on our employee's work to ensure that it's correct? How many times do you find yourself not delegating something because "I can do it better or faster?" Trust plays a significant role in one's ability to live an enjoyable life and get things done.

On the personal side, building trust is the key to your personal brand. Now, I'm no saint; I'm human. I've dished out my share of misery and heartache to others. And, as I made my way through my earlier years, I did some things of which I'm not proud. As I've matured, I've thought deeply about my own missteps and foibles. And, as I explored, it became clear to me that, regardless of the circumstances, there is no excuse for violating the trust of others. The impact of trust-breaking actions is significant.

As I've interacted with many professionals over the years, I've remained amazed at the lack of trust that exists between doctors and their employees. When asking about such critical business development processes as sharing financial data, I'm told that employees don't need that information or can't be trusted with it. The majority of staff members are required to obtain approval for the most mundane purchases. And patients have to jump through a series of hoops in order to obtain a refund or satisfaction on a mishandled action. We don't think enough about the meaning of trust and its impact on our brand — business and personal.

Contrast this distrust with Hyatt, which authorizes even the housekeeping staff with spending up to $2,000 to satisfy a customer. Or how about Nordstrom? Their employee manual is distilled down to one sentence: "Use good judgment in all situations."[1] Talk about efficient and effective!

What is the Cost of Mistrust?

In his book, *The Speed of Trust,* Stephen M.R. Covey tells us that trust is the "one thing that changes everything." He goes on to explain that the economics of trust is clear: as trust increases, the speed at which we get things done also improves, and the cost of doing business goes down. The inverse is also true; as trust goes down, organizations slow down and the cost of doing business increases dramatically.[2]

What impact does trust have on your brand? In today's world, with patients posting reviews on hundreds of sites before they even leave your office, one single trust violation can turn into tens of thousands of dollars in lost revenue — and even the loss of your business.

As I've experienced diverse cultures, it's been interesting to note the difference between our United States and other parts of the world. So much of our cultural differences can be distilled down to this one word: trust.

---

1 Ashley Lutz, "Nordstrom's Employee Handbook Has Only One Rule." *Business Insider*, 10 13, 2014. http://www.businessinsider.com/nordstroms-employee-handbook-2014-10.

2 Stephen M. R. Covey and Rebecca R. Merrill, *The Speed of Trust: The One Thing That Changes Everything* (Free Press, 2008).

Trust is the result of competence and character. If you know your stuff, people will trust you. If you do what you say you will do, people will trust you. If you help your team members develop and learn from mistakes, they'll trust you. If you take care of your patients' needs, they'll trust you and your brand. In business and in your personal life, the degree to which you are trusted will determine what you are able to achieve.

Likewise, your ability to trust others will make a significant difference in your organizational achievements. If your staff feels that they aren't trusted, they will not strive for improvement. If they feel micromanaged or fear making mistakes, they will not innovate.

Remember what I shared with you earlier in the book about William McKnight, the founder of 3M, who believed "Management that is destructively critical when mistakes are made kills initiative, and it's essential that we have many people with initiative if we are to continue to grow."[3]

And so, I ask you: are you creating an environment where people can make mistakes safely and learn from them? An environment where they're allowed to innovate? And are you allowing yourself to be an innovator? To take some risks?

Innovation — at every level — involves risk. Organizations with a reasonable degree of risk tolerance are those that achieve

---

3 "Resources, History, McKnight Principles." 3M Company Information. http://solutions.3m.com/wps/portal/3M/en_US/3M-Company/Information/Resources/History/?PC_Z7_RJH9U52300V200IP896S2Q3223000000_assetId=1319210372704.

breakthroughs. Leaders have to trust those around them. And if you can't, it's better to sever the relationship than to mistrust.

"Nothing is as fast as the speed of trust. Nothing is as fulfilling as a relationship of trust. Nothing is as inspiring as an offering of trust. Nothing is as profitable as the economics of trust, and nothing has more influence than a reputation of trust."[4]

---

4 Covey and Merrill, *The Speed of Trust.*

CHAPTER 24

Change is Your Friend

When I first entered the eye care industry back in 1972, the first plastic spectacle lenses and the first soft contact lenses were being widely introduced. To say that these products revolutionized our industry would be an understatement. Today, these technologies are the standard, and they've evolved through multiple generations of product development.

Throughout the '70s, one of the leading forces in our industry was Corning Glass. They produced the raw materials from which most lenses were made. Today, while still an amazingly innovative company, Corning has very little presence in our industry.

Just 30 years ago, most optometrists could not diagnose or treat disease; they were refractionists who referred their pathologies to ophthalmologists. Today, the vast majority of optometrists are qualified medical practitioners who refer only surgery to ophthalmologists.

Twenty years ago, the technology investment of an optometrist was a single refraction lane, a tonometer, a slit lamp, and a keratometer. An entire optometry practice could be equipped for a relatively small investment. Today, the investment levels have increased exponentially; a high-performing optometrist works out of four lanes of equipment, and technology investments are one of their highest expenses.

Just 10 years ago, a patient with a complaint or compliment might have told a few friends. Today, such communications can be in the hands of thousands before the patient leaves your office.

And today, a patient can get their Rx from an iPhone app and order eyewear with just a few clicks of their mouse.

It doesn't take much insight to realize that the world is evolving rapidly. As a leader, you have to decide where you will stand on the subject of change. Are you going to be the early adopter who leads the charge with the latest technology, the most up-to-date systems, the best trained staff, and the most beautiful building? Are you going to live your life on the bleeding edge?

Or are you going to hold back and keep operating with yesterday's technology, waiting to see how others handle the change?

Back in the fall of 1985, Microsoft introduced Windows. Within a month, Cleinman Performance Partners (with four employees at the time) purchased and installed Windows. The results were disastrous. Simply stated, the first versions of Windows didn't work. Our team put in extra time and energy to get what we needed out of our system, but it was neither fun nor pretty.

As I reflected on the experience, I knew that we wanted to be leading edge; we wanted to have the very best technology available for our team and use it to improve productivity. But I also knew that being too far out front comes at a price. Sometimes, the early adopters get burned. As a result, I defined my firm's technology policy:

> **At Cleinman Performance Partners, we will always be on the ass end of the front end of technology.**

So, what does this have to do with change? Our approach to change is relatively simple. As a firm, we are change agents. We help our clients bring about change in their organizations and in their lives. But, like the technology policy birthed from our Windows experience, we know that, as a small firm, we can't afford significant mistakes. Likewise, neither can our clients. Thus, we invest heavily in understanding what works — and what doesn't. We avoid theoretical approaches and seek the proven. While innovation is a huge part of our culture, most of our innovation comes from two places: first, we borrow it from other industries that have already proven its efficacy. And second, we borrow on our many years of experience to reinvent, redefine, and reevaluate.

So, how does this all relate to you? Change is inevitable. Change opens up opportunities for those who can see it coming. But change is rarely revolutionary. Change evolves. And successful leaders always have their eyes open to trends, their ears open to the members of their team doing the actual work, and their hearts open to customers communicating their needs.

Other chapters in this book deal with the importance of good data. Measuring your practice's performance and monitoring the impact of change is critical to success. Hiring people comfortable with change — indeed, those who lead change — will result in a strategic advantage for you and your practice. The bottom line is that the world is changing around you. You can either harness this change as your friend or suffer the consequences of waking up one day outflanked by your competition.

The owners of Smith Corona, Blockbuster, Circuit City, Kodak, and scores of other businesses are still wondering, "What happened?"

CHAPTER 25

An Equation for Abundance

Over the past four decades, I've had the pleasure of interacting with many thousands of optometrists. Perhaps uniquely so, my interactions have been almost exclusively focused on the business side of optometry and what makes my clients tick. Rarely do I have a discussion about the science of the profession — mostly because I'm simply not qualified to discuss the latest glaucoma treatment or the impact of a particular drop on dry eye. Further, my reality is that these types of issues aren't what motivate me.

I'm far more interested in understanding my clients as people and helping them achieve their goals, both professionally and personally. My work has allowed me to study deeply the people who make up the profession. And during my now 43-year tenure in the industry through more than 20 businesses and scores of products and services, I've had the great fortune to work with many outstanding individuals — fascinating people from whom I've learned and continue to learn much. So far, I've managed to live an abundant life full of challenges, innovation, and meaningful relationships. And for that I am both proud and humble. I've also screwed up royally from time to time and have caused my share of pain for others. And, for that, I am truly sorry yet reflective and thankful for the resulting lessons.

As I thought about how I would close this book, I considered my own legacy. Defining legacy as "that which we leave behind," I've thought about achievement — mine and others. I've considered the differences between the haves and the have nots. I've contemplated the qualities of those professionals whom I consider superstars and of those for whom the struggle seems never-ending. What has emerged for me is a sort of formula — I'm calling it an equation. An equation for the journey to achievement — the attaining of abundance.

Business — and life in general — is tough. As the saying goes, "Dying is easy; it's living that's hard." Just when you think you've got things figured out, something changes. When the moment arrives that you feel you've got the right team doing the right things in the right way, a key player resigns. Almost to the day when you finally achieve the cash flow that you desire, some disaster hits. There are never enough resources, and every plan has at least one hiccup, often many. Every day, in scores of ways, each of us is challenged by both outside influences and our own head trash. Like the tides, life rolls in and out. And like ocean waves, the challenges keep coming and coming. As with the ocean, you should never turn your back on life. Business — like life — is never done until it's done.

On the flip side, opportunities appear almost daily to those with open minds. At the point where one seemingly has few options, the answer magically appears. You meet someone on a plane with a solution. You come across an article that provides key information. When your bank account is running on fumes, along comes more fuel. The reality is that, just when you think that nothing more could go wrong, the tide turns. I know this for a fact. It's happened to me on countless occasions. With an open mind, the answers always appear. Always!

As I've thought about the trials and tribulations of being an entrepreneur, running a business, leading people, innovation, and my own legacy, it has become clear to me that there really is an equation for success. I share it with you for your consideration and as a summary of my overall message in this book.

> **"AN EQUATION FOR ABUNDANCE"**
>
> + You will always have change in your life. Change is your friend.
> + You will always have more challenges than resources. And that's OK.
> + You will always have more opportunities than energy. Choose wisely.
> + You can't go it alone. Don't burn bridges.
> + You will always have assistance available. Look for it.
> + And you will always achieve success if, and only if:
>   - = You don't give up
>   - = You celebrate your blessings
>   - = You never stop seeking to understand
>   - = You never take anything for granted
>   - = You never take yourself too seriously; and
>   - = You express gratitude to those who have helped you.

It is my core belief that the difference between those who are truly successful and those who are destined for struggle can be distilled down to a factor of a few percentage points of extra effort.

Successful individuals exhibit a little more patience and a bit of additional intestinal fortitude. They ask one more question, turn over one more rock. They say "thank you" one more time. They believe that persistence, as Calvin Coolidge once said, is "omnipotent."

> *"Nothing in the world can take the place of persistence. Talent will not; nothing is more common than unsuccessful men with talent. Genius will not; unrewarded genius is almost a proverb. Education will not; the world is full of educated derelicts. Persistence and determination alone are omnipotent.[1]*

Truly successful people are never done. Why would you want to be?

---

1 *Respectfully Quoted: A Dictionary of Quotations. 1989* (Attributed to Calvin Coolidge). http://www.bartleby.com/73/1355.html

ACKNOWLEDGEMENTS

This final chapter provides me with the opportunity to tell a few stories that all add up to how I've come to this place in my life, having spent the past 43 years in the eye care industry. You've come this far and I'm hoping that you won't now get bored. What I'm going to share will help you understand a bit of what makes this entrepreneur tick.

The publishing of this book starts me on a new journey in my life. While I've been writing for several decades — turning out literally hundreds of articles and papers, plans, and reports — this is my first real book. I don't think it will be my last.

I started this project in May of 2009 while on a beach vacation in Rockport, Massachusetts. The weather was horrible, so I started to write, and I've been working on the project off and on for the past six years. Some chapters may be recognizable, as they've been previously published in my blog at www.cleinman. com, while others you may have experienced in some form in such magazines as *Optometric Management* and *Eyecare Business*. Hopefully, I've struck a chord or two with this collection of thoughts and observations. In terms of acknowledgements, it is my readers and audience I must first thank. It is through your comments over the years about my various writings that have encouraged me to keep going. Thank you.

As a group, I want to thank my clients for your assistance. Since 1979, I've worked almost exclusively with private practice optometrists — originally as co-founder of the first national buying group, Co-Optics of America, and then, beginning in 1989, as a consultant, writer, speaker, and leader through Cleinman Performance Partners. Along the way, I've had the opportunity to work intimately with some of North America's finest and most successful optometrists and their teams. I've learned much from them and thank them for the opportunity to be their trusted advisor.

I must also acknowledge my team members. Since the founding of my first real business in 1979, I've had the pleasure of working side by side with an incredible group of talented individuals. You've challenged me to continuously improve my leadership and business skills. You've provided insight that I would never have otherwise seen. You've set me straight when I've missed the mark. Together, we've celebrated success and reflected on failure. I recognize that working for a creative, opinionated, and high-energy entrepreneur isn't easy. But you've never been bored. Thank you for your hard work, patience, and loyalty. Thanks also to Kathleen Avery, Johanna Loeffler, Ginamarie Wells, Nancy Furdock, Rosemarie Feudi, Adrienne Wise, Amanda Van Voris, Judith Lee, and all the others who helped me complete this book.

There are a number of individuals whom I must acknowledge for their profound contribution to my career and, as a result, to this book.

First, I must thank my parents, Helen and Max Cleinman. As small-town grocers, antique dealers, and purveyors of such diverse products as shoes and Thin Mints, they worked tirelessly to deliver their services to our community. Together with my grandparents, they taught me how to work and how to take pride in what I accomplish. While no longer with us, their influence on my life has been profound and I miss them dearly.

My first employer, Jack Rumery, provided me with two important life lessons. A descendant of the founder of Gilbertsville, New York, the tiny village where I grew up, Jack lived in a huge house on a beautiful estate that contained our little village's only private tennis court and swimming pool. When I was the ripe age of 10, Jack provided me with an equation that has had profound impact on my life:

Hard Work = Reward

One fall day, I raked some leaves for him, which resulted in my very first paycheck — for eight dollars. I can still see that check in my mind's eye. I went on to become Jack's yard boy and worked for him for about four years. Along the way, Jack also taught me benevolence. You see, Jack allowed many of our village's children to use his tennis court and swimming pool. He was a generous man who contributed much to our community. He set an example that I'll never forget. Thank you, Jack.

Acknowledgements

I'm often asked how it was that I arrived in the eye care industry, a relationship I've passionately enjoyed since I was just 16. As with many things in life, it was the result of a confluence of forces. First, as a well-known young hustler in my community who was always seeking an opportunity to trade good work for a buck, I was offered a job selling popcorn at a local racetrack at age 13. It was through popcorn that I first met Dr. Bill Lusk, an optometrist who sponsored one of the stock cars. Bill was a regular Friday night popcorn customer — always good for a nickel commission and sometimes even a nice tip. Coincidently, he and his family had just moved to the little village that I called home, having purchased an incredible property right next to the Rumery home where I could be seen mowing the lawn. Bill subsequently hired me as his yard boy and, for the next couple of years, we had many an adventure. I was both a tireless worker and surrogate son — available at almost any hour. Bill had the energy of three men and worked two jobs — one as an optometrist with a successful practice and the other restoring his estate to its prior glory.

Now, Bill was (and is to this day) a creative man. He had gone into the frame distribution business, securing the United States distributorship for a German line. He operated Brillen Optical out of his office basement and sold his wares through mail order, sending color postcards to optometrists and opticians nationwide. Being in the popcorn business at an early age and having entrepreneurial parents, I enjoyed talking business. I knew my numbers — how much a box of popcorn cost me and what my profit margin was. Bill and I often talked about his side business, and one day I suggested to Bill that his mail pieces might prove more successful if followed up by phone. The rest, as the saying goes, is history. I soon found myself — one month into my 16th year — selling frames via telephone to optometrists and opticians around the nation. I would hitchhike the 20 miles from my school to Bill's office and work in the basement. Seated at half of a ping pong table and using a rotary wall phone, I'd dial for dollars. I'd make calls from 4:00 p.m. until 7:00 p.m., pitching my wares following the time zones west. I was successful and made my employer money (earning $1.50 an hour for myself). During my last two years of high school, I became one of the first individuals to engage in a work-study program, working full time and taking college courses at night. I actually flew home from the American Optometric Association's national convention to graduate from high school.

From ages 16 to 23, I worked alongside Dr. Lusk as his first salesman, then national sales manager, operations manager and, ultimately, director of marketing. As a member of a four-person management team, I learned about business operations and our industry from the ground up. I was a salesman and I managed salespeople. I helped develop picking, packing, and invoicing systems; implemented advertising campaigns; designed trade show booths; and handled industry relations. I installed a print shop and designed and produced our own catalogs. At the age of 18, I even helped secure an investment in the company. I hired and fired, created and executed. And I learned.

Acknowledgements

So, why this long story to say thanks? Imagine how unique it was that any individual would give a 16-year-old the opportunity that Bill Lusk gave me. Bill opened the door for me to a career, a life's passion, and countless adventures. I can only imagine how my life would have unfolded had I followed my first career path — that of a gardener.

Bill Lusk — optometrist and entrepreneur, friend and employer — thank you for believing in me. Your confidence (or naiveté) is something for which I am profoundly grateful. Through your actions and support, you delivered to me another valuable life lesson — one which I continually employ: keep your eyes and your mind open; one never knows from whom a unique opportunity will arise.

During my tenure with Brillen Optical, I had occasion to meet Thomas Schinkel, a young international business consultant. The former managing director of the Dutch Wholesaler's Association, Thomas had immigrated to the United States to obtain his MBA from Ohio State and worked with a variety of European firms, including a Swedish frame manufacturer seeking a United States distributor. We were successful in landing that business opportunity, during which time I had my first dealings with a consultant. I was enamored by Tom's perspective and approach and, for a small town boy growing up in an insulated and isolated world, his Dutch accent. I distinctly remember that day in 1977 when I said to myself, "Someday, I want to be a consultant like Tom."

A Different Perspective

As I entered my 20s — married and contemplating a family — I became increasingly desirous of running my own show. Independence was, after all, in my blood. Just after my 23rd birthday, following the purchase of my first home and with my first child on the way, I decided to embark on my own. I had a killer idea for a new type of frame importing firm. I was certain of riches beyond my imagination.

Having read the book *How to Borrow Your Way to a Great Fortune,*[1] I walked into several banks on the same day and completed loan applications at each (to technically avoid lying about my obligations). It worked! Now, armed with $10,000 (my salary at the time was $18,000) in borrowed funds and an idea, I drove to Boston to tap into the brilliance that was Tom Schinkel. Now, Tom is the smartest man I know. Yet, despite his intelligence, he agreed to help me. Together, we spun my original hair-brained scheme into what became Co-Optics of America, the granddaddy of the buying group industry. Tom and I, as partners, launched that firm and worked side by side for five years through many adventures, plowing new ground for an entirely new industry segment. I ultimately bought Tom's interest, and he went on to become a leading worldwide expert in the office products industry, a position that he holds to this day. I thank Tom for his support of my scheme, for our many adventures together, and for teaching me some of the fundamentals of planning and analysis. I consider Tom to be one of my very best friends and am eternally grateful for his mentorship. I thank

---

1 Gregory Tyler Hicks, *How to Borrow Your Way to a Great Fortune* (New York: Parker Pub., 1970).

Tom also for helping me prove out another life lesson: what you can dream, you can accomplish.

Finally, I honor an individual who has had a profound impact on my current business, although the roots of our relationship go way back to the early days of Co-Optics of America.

I'm always enamored of individuals who take bold steps, bring about change, and help lift us all to new heights. It is through the creativity and passion of these individuals that we enjoy the new technologies, equipment, instruments, fashion, systems, and methodologies upon which we all rely. They put the food on our table. They take the risks that others will not.

I first met Dr. Ron Blum when he became associated with Co-Optics back in 1980 as member number 41. At the time, he was a practicing optometrist with a single location which he had just purchased. He went on to become a columnist on marketing for *20/20 Magazine* and ultimately built one of the largest multi-location optometry practices in the nation. I knew he was a special individual when he asked Tom Schinkel and I for our opinion of an invention of his — a special shoelace additive that would prevent his kids' shoes from coming untied. Seems he hated wasting time. Called "TIE TITES," while not likely a commercial success, this was the first of literally hundreds of patents awarded to this amazing genius. In the late 1980s, he turned his attention to lenses and was instrumental in creating and patenting technology that was the foundation of the in-office lens casting movement.

A Different Perspective

In early 1989, I had made the decision to retire from Co-Optics, having sold majority interest to a group of venture capitalists. I was seeking new challenges and, frankly, I didn't enjoy working for an investment and investors. I wanted to help others and spend more time with my young family. I knew that it was time for me to fulfill the dream that I'd uncovered more than a dozen years prior with my first exposure to Tom Schinkel. I wanted to consult. I issued a press release announcing my pending retirement and, just prior to Vision Expo, *Vision Monday* ran a short article entitled "Cleinman quits Co-Optics to become Consultant." My phone rang. At the end of the line was Dr. Ron Blum — optometrist/inventor/entrepreneur. Ron and two colleagues were seeking some assistance with suppliers and I was uniquely qualified to help. Ron's practice became Cleinman Performance Partners' Client Number One.

As the leader of his multi-location practice, Ron belonged to a small study group of similar-sized practices that met semiannually to share ideas and solutions. In January of 1990, I was invited by Ron to make a presentation to this group about some of the work I was doing for Ron's practice and that of his two business associates. It was through Ron's support that the majority of these individuals retained me to assist them and their practices. For the first decade of our firm's history, I was deeply engaged in strategic and operational development for some of optometry's most successful practices; names like Fuller, Halpern, McDougall, Ossip, Schaeffer, Bolick, and Samit formed the foundation of Cleinman Performance Partners' client base.

Acknowledgements

Their group was one of the inspirations for today's Cleinman Performance Network, which now represents hundreds of North America's most successful optometry practices.

Ron later went on to conceive Innotech, a firm with which I'm proud to have been associated as one of five founders, its first CFO, and a director. As a consultant, I helped to recruit its original management team and secure its first round of financing. I negotiated licenses and dealt with intellectual property rights. I wrote business plans and negotiated supply agreements. The firm ultimately went public and was subsequently acquired by Johnson & Johnson. Ron later founded The Egg Factory, a technology development firm. He also founded PixelOptics and more than a dozen other firms and technologies — and he's not done. Thomas Edison has 1,093 patents to his name. My prediction is that Ron Blum will approach that milestone. Needless to say, the man is an idea machine and a tireless worker. He's one of the few people who have returned my 3:00 a.m. emails instantly.

So, it is with profound gratitude that I thank Dr. Ron Blum for his support and partnership and for the many doors that he's opened for me over the past 35 years.

Each of the individuals I have mentioned — along with countless others — has made a significant contribution to my personal development as a businessman and member of society. Each of their own careers can be summarized by a poem by Dean Alfange that I have in my office which lays forth much of what I believe about life:

"It is my right to be uncommon — if I can. I seek opportunity — not security... I want to take the calculated risk; to dream and to build, to fail and to succeed. I refuse to barter incentive for a dole. I prefer the challenges of life to the guaranteed existence; the thrill of fulfillment to the stale calm of utopia. I will not trade my freedom for beneficence nor my dignity for a handout. I will never cower before any master nor bend to any threat. It is my heritage to stand erect, proud and unafraid; to think and act for myself, enjoy the benefit of my creations, and to face the world boldly and say, this I have done."[2]

To the many hundreds of clients I have worked with over the years; to the countless industry and business connections I have made (especially Barney Dougher, President of Hoya, who has so generously supported our work); to my friends and to those with whom I've shared my life; to my children and siblings, cousins and classmates, teachers and tutors; to all who have touched me in so many profound ways so far on my journey, thank you from the bottom of my heart.

Stay tuned... I'm not done yet.

---

2 *Respectfully Quoted: A Dictionary of Quotations.* 1989. (Dean Alfange, creed). http://www.bartleby.com/73/71.html.

NOTES

NOTES